Discover Christ

Developing a Personal
Relationship with Jesus

Discover Christ

Developing a Personal
Relationship with Jesus

Bert Ghezzi and Dave Nodar

Our Sunday Visitor Publishing Division
Our Sunday Visitor, Inc.
Huntington, Indiana 46750

Nihil Obstat:
Msgr. Michael Heintz, Ph.D.
Censor Librorum

Imprimatur:
✠ Kevin C. Rhoades
Bishop of Fort Wayne-South Bend
August 23, 2011

The *Nihil Obstat* and *Imprimatur* are declarations that a work is free from doctrinal or moral error. It is not implied that those who have granted the *Nihil Obstat* and *Imprimatur* agree with the contents, opinions, or statements expressed.

ISBN 978-1-59276-030-5 (Inventory No. T1179)
LCCN: 2011933381

Interior design by M. Urgo
Cover design by Amanda Falk
Cover photo by Shutterstock

PRINTED IN THE UNITED STATES OF AMERICA

Contents

Introduction

You have opened a book that invites you to discover Christ — a book that offers to help you enter into or renew more fully a personal relationship with Jesus.

Curiosity may have prompted you to pick it up. Or *Discover Christ* may connect with a longing that you have been feeling. Or maybe a relative or friend handed the book to you, saying something like, "This book has meant a lot to me. I think you may like it, too."

Whatever occasioned your picking up *Discover Christ,* we encourage you to read it with an open mind and heart. Many of the chapters challenge you to respond to pivotal questions that you may (or may not) have already considered. Questions like "What is the meaning of life?" and "Why does Jesus matter?" We call

Discover Christ is based on *Discovering Christ,* a video-driven, interactive course developed and distributed by ChristLife, a ministry in the Archdiocese of Baltimore. Please turn to the back pages of the book for information about ChristLife and *Discovering Christ.*

them "pivotal" because they demand answers that can turn lives around or, perhaps, right-side up.

We tell you at the beginning of each chapter whether it was written by Bert or Dave. Throughout the book, we share how we came to discover Christ and to relate to him personally. We tell you about our experiences because both of us discovered Christ through conversations with friends. May our example be a source of encouragement for you to meet him in these pages.

Chapter One

What Is the Meaning of Life?

Dave

Asking the Question

When God was creating the different creatures, he first created the dog. He told the dog, "Look, I want you to sit at your house at the door, and I want you to bark like crazy when anybody goes by or when they walk in. I'm going to give you a life span of twenty years." The dog said, "Lord, that's pretty rough, twenty years of barking. Could you make it ten and I'll give you back ten?" The Lord said, "Agreed."

Next the Lord created a monkey. He said to the monkey, "I want you to entertain people. I want you to do tricks for them and make them laugh. For this, I will give you a life span of twenty years." The monkey, like the dog, said, "Lord, you know, that's quite a gig, to have twenty years to make people laugh and do tricks for them. Could I ask you to give me a ten-year life span, and I'll give you ten back just like the dog did?" The Lord agreed.

Next the Lord created a cow. He said to the cow, "I want you to go out into the fields, into the pastures, with the farmer, under the hot sun and I want you to toil with him, eat grass. I want you to have calves, and I want you to provide milk for the farmer's family. And I want you to live a life span of sixty years." The cow said, "That's a long time, Lord. Could you cut that down? How about if I have twenty years and I give you back forty?" The Lord agreed.

Then the Lord created man, and he said to the man, "I want to give you a life where you eat, sleep, play, marry, and enjoy your life. For this, I'll give you twenty years." The man said, "Ah, Lord, only twenty years? Could you possibly give me my twenty, the forty years from the cow, the monkey's ten, and the ten the dog gave back? That makes eighty, okay?" The Lord agreed.

So that is why for our first twenty years we eat, sleep, play, and enjoy ourselves. For the next forty years, we slave to support our families. For the next ten years, we do monkey tricks for the grandchildren. And for the last ten years, we sit on the front porch and bark at everyone.

We laugh at this joke because it tells truths about us with a touch of humor. Our lives do go through the stages it describes. But when we are done laughing, we may begin to wonder about the dullness of lives that move along without any apparent sense of purpose. For me the joke opened the question of the meaning of life, and I want to open it for you.

Imagine that I stop you walking on Main Street, put a microphone up to your face, and ask, "Would you mind taking a minute to answer an important question?" "Okay with me," you say. And so I ask, "What is the meaning of life to you?" Off the top of your head, what would you say? You may have already thought about your life's purpose and hit the nail on the head. But maybe like many of us you have never confronted the question of life's meaning. Consider these wildly diverse responses to the same question my friend Pete put to people he met recently in downtown Baltimore, Maryland:

**Pete, with roving microphone in hand:
"What is the meaning of life to you?"**

"I kind of gauge it as finding peace within yourself and happiness. I mean, I think people have many different ideas of how to go about finding happiness but think it's all these little trivial things. Ultimately it's just finding what's within because then you can be happy wherever you are. It's internal. That's my best guess."
— *Twenty-something woman*

"Living these days being a responsible human being. You know, I raised my kids right.

They're in college now, and I'm tryin' to do right with the rest of my life."
— *Dad with grown children*

"Well, what Judaism says is the purpose of mankind is to get closer to God. And, so, things that people do that are positive help them get closer to God. And, so, from a religious spiritual point of view, that's what the meaning of life is. And there's multiple other meanings at a much lower level than that, but that's the spiritual answer to your question."
— *Middle-aged man*

"Having fun. Go do bad things, good things, [friend laughing in the background] but, uh, live your life. Try doing anything you want to do."
— *Late-teen youth*

"The meaning of life is doing what the Lord asks us to do. And fulfilling whatever He asks us to do."
— *Young man*

"That can be hard to answer because it's something you would have to think about. Maybe it's God's decision, it might be some other belief, but it really is not an easy question."
— *Elderly man*

Not an easy question, to be sure, but one that we must answer because how our life turns out depends upon it. People have wrestled with it for centuries. Philosophers, nurses, teachers, plumbers, flight attendants, lawyers, construction workers — all at some point have had to wonder, "Why am I here? and "Where am I headed?"

I recently read an article by a professor who bemoaned the fact that colleges and universities are so committed to research that they no longer expose students to the important questions about life. But in the past even grade schools taught kids about life's meaning. For example, I attended a Catholic elementary school. In the third grade I had to memorize a lesson about the purpose of life. My religion book posed the question, "Why did God create you?" And it gave the answer that I was expected to commit to memory. Today I can still repeat it. But not until my late teen years did I confront the important question of my life's meaning as a real issue.

Facing the Issue

For most of us the issue of our purpose lurks beneath the surface of our super-busy lives. But then something happens that makes it pop up. For some of us, the example of a friend living a peaceful, purpose-driven life provokes curiosity about our own lack of direction. For others, a joyous event like the birth of a child or the marriage of a beloved daughter opens them to reflect all teary-eyed on life's meaning.

But more often a crisis compels us to ask what's really going on in our lives. The question may arise while we are struggling with addiction, depression, loneliness, or thoughts of suicide. The weight of guilt or shame for some offensive behavior may force us to ask what life is about. Or serious disease or financial collapse may make us wonder about the meaning of life. In fact, you may be facing one of these crises right now.

Sometimes a broader crisis such as a natural disaster — maybe an earthquake, hurricane, or flood — does the job. Or a national catastrophe like an assassination or a terrorist attack may rouse us to look at reality. For example, the September 11, 2001, collapse of the World Trade Center awakened many Americans to consider life's purpose.

Anesthetizing the Pain

Until we have a wake-up call, many of us plod along realizing that we haven't found what we're looking for. A longing gnaws at us, a pain even, a sense that there's got to be more to life than what we're experiencing. We feel an emptiness deep inside like a gaping hole that must be filled.

Until we have a wake-up call, many of us plod along realizing that we haven't found what we're looking for.

So we look for ways to anesthetize our pain. We may seek comfort in relationships or dream that marriage and a family will do it. We may imagine that becoming successful and acquiring a lot of money will make us happy. We may look to physical fitness, beauty, or achievement in sports for relief. We may try to fill the hole inside us by medicating ourselves with drugs or alcohol. Or we may just try to ignore it by having fun.

That's what I did in my teenage years. I thought that having fun, entertaining others, and relating to girls was my life's purpose. I played guitar in rock and roll groups that were fairly successful in Baltimore. But none of this satisfied me. For example, once, surrounded by friends at a really good party — good by my standards at the time — I found myself thinking that there's got to be a better party somewhere. I was just ignoring the hole. Nothing I was doing even began to cure the ache I felt in my heart.

> **I think everybody should get rich and famous and do everything they ever dreamed of so they can see that that's not the answer.**
>
> *— Jim Carrey*[1]

The Inevitability of Death

Screenwriter Woody Allen once quipped that he isn't afraid of dying. He then went on to say he just doesn't want to be there when it happens. We chuckle at the joke, but when we confront the inevitability of our own death, we take the matter seriously. Recognizing the inescapable fact that we will die may bring to the surface critical questions about life's meaning: Why am I here? Where did I come from? Where am I going?

For example, Leo Tolstoy, in *A Confession,* tells how he came close to committing suicide because a sense of purposelessness tormented him. "Is there any

Death Scared the Hell Out of Me

"I was just doing my own thing and thinking that life is just life and you have to make the best of it.

"Everything changed one day for me as I sat in my English class during my junior year in high school. We were reading the play *Our Town,* a three-act play by Thornton Wilder. It's a pretty simple play, but it had a not-so-simple impact on my life at the time. At the end of the play one of the main characters, Emily Webb, dies. While in the graveyard with the other people who are dead there, she asks them if she could go back and relive a day in her life….

"The play encourages people to really live life and not to miss the little things. But what hit me as a seventeen-year-old kid was that I was going to die some day. And it scared the hell, literally, right out of me. I started to shake in the class and to sweat; I began thinking: "Oh my God, I'm going to die. So what is the meaning of life? Is there any meaning? Is there anything after death?"

— *Fr. Larry Richards*[2]

meaning in life," he asked, "that will not be annihilated by the inevitability of death that awaits me?"[3] And having come to the verge of self-destruction, he began a quest for meaning. He searched in the sciences and in philosophy, but found that they had nothing to offer. Ultimately to his surprise he found the answer in the peasants who worked for him on his estate. These simple folks discovered their life's meaning in their Christian faith. So Tolstoy gradually came to believe that he found his purpose in the person of Jesus Christ.

Finding Our Purpose

Like it did for Tolstoy, facing the inevitability of death should provoke us to explore the purpose of life. And as we think about the matter we must confront an "either/or" fact: everything in reality is *either* an accident *or* has been created for a purpose. "There are only two ways," says author Frank Sheed, "in which anything can come to be. Either it's intentional or accidental; that is, either someone intended it or it merely happened

> **Humanity, like other things, must either be an accident and so purposeless, or else have been made with intent.**
>
> — *Frank Sheed*

by chance. The thing that is intentional has a purpose; accidents have no purpose. Humanity, like other things, must either be an accident and so purposeless, or else have been made with intent."[4]

If you are looking at something that was made and that is obviously not an accident, you must figure out what it was made for. You must understand its purpose.

For example, in Daytona Beach, Florida, a toddler found a hand grenade in a field near his home. He apparently thought it was a toy. His dad found him playing with it, took it and gave it to the police. "Thank God he didn't pull the plug," the dad said.[5]

We will never use something correctly until we discover what it was made to do. This general principle applies to all created things. If we don't know a thing's purpose, we will misuse it with unhappy, even potentially disastrous results, as the example suggests. The principle also applies to human beings. If we do not come to understand our purpose, we will never satisfy our longings or find happiness. We must look beyond ourselves to discover what we are and why we were made. And for many of us this requires a revolution in how we look at our lives.

A Radical Shift in Worldview

At some time or other, all of us behave as though everything revolves around us. We are convinced that we get to decide the meaning of life for ourselves. For example, some of the people on the street that Peter interviewed said that their purpose is enjoying life, having fun, and doing whatever they wanted. We all need to change the way we see reality. We must come to a genuine understanding of the meaning of our existence. We must finally recognize who and what we are, where we have come from, and where we are going.

To do this, we need an astronomical shift in our personal worldview like the astronomical shift — literally — that Copernicus brought about in the view of the world. From the second century on everyone accepted the scientific opinion of Ptolemy, the Egyptian astronomer, who held that the sun revolved around the earth. But in the sixteenth century Copernicus, the great Polish astronomer, developed the theory, later proven, that the earth revolved around

We need an astronomical shift in our personal worldview like the astronomical shift — literally — that Copernicus brought about in the view of the world.

the sun. Similarly, we must stop seeing ourselves at the center of things. We must shed the notion that we are self-determined beings and accept the fact that we are creatures. And we must recognize that the intelligent being who created us has given us our purpose.

I said earlier that I still remember the answer I had to memorize for the question, "Why did God create you?" It goes like this: "He created me (and you, too) to know, love, and serve him in this life and to be with him forever in the next." God intended to bring us into a relationship with himself. He designed us to share his own life so that we would enjoy peace and happiness now and forever. He revealed his purpose for us fully in his Son, Jesus Christ, whom he sent into the world to satisfy all our longings. And it is in Jesus that we come to know who God is, understand what he is like, and finally grasp the meaning of life. As one contemporary paraphrase of Scripture declares, "It's in Christ that we find out who we are and what we are living for. Long before we first heard of Christ and got our hopes up, he had his eye on us, had designs on us for glorious living, part of the overall purpose he is working out in every-thing and everyone" (Ephesians 1:11, *The Message*).

We can stop trying subjectively to figure out why we exist because we can learn it in Christ. As the New Testament says, "For everything, absolutely everything, above and below, visible and invisible … — *everything* got started in him and finds it purpose in him" (Colossians 1:16, *The Message*, emphasis added). And Jesus proclaimed his intention for us when he said, "I came that they may have life, and have it abundantly" (John 10:10).

Here is what will bring our lives into proper focus:

- to see our lives as no longer revolving around us;

- to accept that a God who loves us created us;

- to recognize that he wants to reveal himself to us through Jesus Christ; and

- to make the astronomical change of putting him at the center of our lives.

Turning to God

Bert's priest friend Fr. Ed Thompson says that our heaven is to be with God forever, but God's heaven is to be with us forever. God desires to be with us so much, that he makes it easy for us to come into a relationship with him. Scripture says, "… I know the plans I have for you, says the LORD, plans for your welfare and not for harm, to give you a future with hope. Then when you call upon me and come and pray to me, I will hear you" (Jeremiah 29:11–12). If we make even a slight move toward him, he will make a big move toward us. As James promises in his letter, "Draw near to God, and he will draw near to you" (James 4:8).

You don't need to take my word for it. You can say to God, "If what Dave says is true, I ask you to reveal yourself to me."

Chapter Two

Why Does Jesus Matter?

Bert

Popular Views of Jesus

During his public ministry, Jesus asked his hearers many questions, some of which still challenge us today. For example, "Why are you afraid?" (Mark 4:40); "What are you looking for?" (John 1:38); "What do you want me to do for you?" (Matthew 20:32); and "Do you still not understand?" (Matthew 16:9, NJB). And the most important question Jesus asked of his original disciples he now poses to us: "Who do you say that I am?" (Matthew 16:15).

What answer would you give? Take a moment and think about it.

Like the kids on Art Linkletter's "People Are Funny" show, sometimes people say the darndest things when asked about Jesus' identity. Consider the extremes of the answers pedestrians recently gave at a sidewalk interview:

Pete, in downtown Baltimore with roving mike, asking, "Who is Jesus Christ to you?"

"To me it's my higher power."

— *Older man*

"I personally think that Jesus Christ was an influential figure who may or may not have been fictional."

— *Young man*

"Jesus Christ was a great teacher and a great prophet."

— *Young man*

"He is son of a god and someone who can save this world."

— *Older man*

"A good person we can all look forward to meeting when we die."

— *Young woman*

"A figment of most people's imagination. As far as Jesus Christ's concerned, your opinion is as good as mine."

— *Young man*

"A beautiful role model ... an excellent kind of idea to live by."

— *Young woman*

Our answer to "Who is Jesus Christ?" draws a line across our lives. As you will see, what we believe about him can shape our lives.

People typically say that Jesus was a "good man," "a great teacher," or "an excellent role model." All of these views contain a germ of truth, but none of them adequately express Jesus' true identity.

If Jesus were merely a *good man*, we probably would never have heard of him. Millions of good women and men have made substantial contributions to their societies and have remained unknown. A few good people have achieved world historical status, but no one rivals the cosmic influence of Jesus. No, "good man" does not begin to describe him.

Neither does *great teacher* adequately identify Jesus. The world has seen many great teachers, and we have ignored most of them. For example, the Greek philosopher Plotinus (A.D. 205–270) enjoyed the reputation as a great teacher, but I doubt anyone today calls himself a Plotinian. The world cannot ignore Jesus even if it wanted to because he was more than a great teacher. No mere teacher has affected billions of people and shaped the course of human events as Jesus has.

People sometimes say that Jesus came to show us how to live a good life. For example, one young woman Pete interviewed claimed that he was "a beautiful role model." If that's what Jesus was about, he apparently set a standard too high for most to attain, one that could lead to frustration rather than success. Like taking Warren Buffett as a good example for our money management and despairing because we can't measure up.

Jesus' Profound Cultural Relevance

Dave

Jesus exercises a profound influence on world culture far beyond that of any ordinary person, no matter how good or great. Consider these evidences of his enduring relevance:

- We regard the birth of Christ as the dividing point in human history. Our calendars mark the years "before Christ" as B.C., and we designate the years after Christ as A.D., which derives from the Latin phrase "*anno domini*," which means "in the year of our Lord."

- The media — print, radio, television, and the Internet — maintain a continual interest in Jesus. Even scurrilous speculations that he married Mary Magdalene, did not die on the cross, or arrived in a UFO cannot explain his lasting popularity. Rather, millions of people sense something deep within their beings that attracts them to Jesus and generates persistent media attention about him.

- The profane use of Jesus' name also demonstrates, although negatively, his relevance in contemporary culture. For example, once a woman that I had not seen since high school was chatting with me and said, "Oh, Dave, do you have any kids?" "Yes, I've got five children," I said. "Jesus Christ!" she exclaimed. And I said, "Exactly!" She shuddered and then shared this anecdote, "You know what? I'm Catholic, too. When my son was five years old we decided to bring him to church for the first time. We were a little late and the church was crowded. As we were squeezing into a pew, he pointed to the crucifix and asked, "Who's that on the cross, Mom?" I said, "Shhh ... it's Jesus Christ." And he said, "Mom, don't say that in here!" True story. We use the Lord's name, Jesus, as a unique swear word in our culture. People don't profane any other names. Think about it. Nobody ever swore using my name or your name. They certainly don't use the names of other religious leaders. You've never heard someone shout "Buddha" in anger or "Mohammed" in disgust. Profaning Jesus' name acknowledges, in a backhanded way, his supreme reality and his profound impact on human history.

What Jesus Did

Although Jesus was a good man, a great teacher, and an excellent moral example, he was about doing something far beyond these mere human callings. People sometimes sum up what Jesus did by saying that he made it possible for us to go to heaven when we die, but that's also only part of a much bigger truth. Jesus changed human history forever. And his intervention into human events made a radical difference for every one of us.

When Jesus began his public ministry he proclaimed the core of his message, revealing what he was doing. The New Testament reports that "Jesus came into Galilee, preaching the good news of God, and saying, 'The time is fulfilled, and the kingdom of God has come near; repent, and believe in the good news'" (Mark 1:14–15). By the arrival of the kingdom of God he meant that God was establishing his rule on earth. The message gradually became clear to all: Jesus was announcing the wondrous truth that God, the Creator of the universe, was working through him to set things right for all humanity.

Jesus demonstrated the reality of the good news by performing significant works that displayed God's power acting through him. For example, Matthew recounted in his gospel that

> **Jesus went throughout Galilee, teaching in their synagogues and proclaiming the good news of the kingdom and curing every disease and every sickness among the people. So his fame spread throughout all Syria, and they brought to him all the sick, those who were**

afflicted with various diseases and pains, demoniacs, epileptics, and paralytics, and he cured them. And great crowds followed him from Galilee, the Decapolis, Jerusalem, Judea, and from beyond the Jordan (Matthew 4:23–25).

Huge crowds gathered around Jesus. They clamored for his attention because they witnessed how he acted with authority to heal the sick and to take command over evil spirits. And Jesus exercised his supernatural powers in ways that made his followers grapple with his identity. He demonstrated his control over nature, his authority over life and death, and his power to forgive sins.

Calming the storm. After a long day and night of nonstop ministry, Jesus and his apostles got into a boat to cross the sea. Overwhelmed with exhaustion, he fell asleep in the bow. Then, as Matthew reported in his gospel, "a windstorm arose on the sea, so great that the boat was being swamped by the waves" (Matthew 8:24). The storm lashed the boat so severely that even the four apostles who were commercial fishermen despaired. Fearing for their lives, they woke Jesus, begging him to save them. He gently corrected them for their lack of faith. "Then he got up and rebuked the winds and the sea," said Matthew, "and there was a dead calm. They were amazed, saying 'What sort of man is this, that even winds and sea obey him?'" (Matthew 8:26–27). The apostles began to suspect that Jesus was not merely a great teacher.

Raising the dead. Jesus' friend Lazarus had died and was in the tomb for four days before Jesus arrived on the scene. Lazarus's sisters Mary and Martha believed that had Jesus been there he would have healed their brother. Jesus assured Martha that Lazarus would rise again. "I am the resurrection and the life," he said to her. "'Those who believe in me, even though they die, will live, and everyone who lives and believes in me will never die. Do you believe this?' She said to him, 'Yes, Lord, I believe that you are the Messiah, the Son of God, the one coming into the world'" (John 11:25–27).

Martha had recognized Jesus' true identity, but evidently did not expect that he could bring Lazarus back to life. For when Jesus commanded that they take away the stone from the grave, she resisted:

> **Martha, the sister of the dead man, said to him, "Lord, already there is a stench because he has been dead four days." Jesus said to her, "Did I not tell you that if you believed, you would see the glory of God?" So they took away the stone. And Jesus looked upward and said, "Father, I thank you for having heard me. I knew that you always hear me, but I have said this for the sake of the crowd standing here, so that they may believe that you sent me." When he had said this, he cried with a loud voice, "Lazarus, come out!" The dead man came out, his hands and feet bound with strips of cloth, and his face wrapped in a cloth. Jesus said to them, "Unbind him, and let him go" (John 11:39–44).**

Jesus had made it plain to all that God was working in and through him to destroy the forces of evil and bring new life to humankind.

Forgiveness of sins. Some men carrying a paralyzed friend to Jesus could not get him through the crowd. Determined to seek their friend's healing, they climbed to the roof, dug through it, and lowered him right in front of Jesus. Mark says that when he saw their faith, "he said to the paralytic, 'Son, your sins are forgiven'" (Mark 2:5). This declaration caused quite a stir among Jewish teachers in the crowd. They regarded it as blasphemy and questioned in their hearts, "Who can forgive sins but God alone?" Jesus read their thoughts and said:

> **"Which is easier, to say to the paralytic, 'Your sins are forgiven,' or to say 'Stand up and take your mat and walk'? But so that you may know that the Son of Man has authority on earth to forgive sins" — he said to the paralytic — "I say to you, stand up, take your mat and go to your home." And he stood up, and immediately took the mat and went out before all of them; so that they were all amazed and glorified God, saying, "We have never seen anything like this!" (Mark 2:9–12).**

No one in the crowd missed the significance of the event. Jesus had forgiven sins, an action that expressed his relationship with God. Jesus, the Son of God, was making his oneness with the Father unmistakably clear. At a later time he explicitly declared his divine Sonship in a conversation with some Jewish leaders when he said, "The Father and I are one" (John 10:30). The Jews immediately took up stones to kill him. Jesus said to them, "'I have shown you many good works from the Father. For which of these are you going to stone me?' The Jews answered, 'It is not for a good work that we are going to stone you, but for blasphemy; because you, though only a human being, are making yourself God'" (John 10:31–33). After defending his work further, he escaped from their hands. Jesus never denied their charge that he was making himself God.

A Rescue Operation

All who encountered Jesus recognized that he was doing something extraordinary. Jesus' miracles persuaded many that God was acting through him to fix humanity's brokenness. That's what Jesus meant when he declared that the kingdom of God had come. At the climax of his ministry, he established God's kingdom by his death and resurrection. Jesus destroyed evil by his death on the cross and he launched the kingdom by his resurrection to new life.

Jesus' rescue operation has a profound significance for each of us. Consider, for example, the effect that Christ's death and resurrection had on St. Paul. He experienced himself as the worst of sinners because he had arrested Christians and approved of the execution of Stephen. Yet Jesus rescued him and gave him new life. "I have been crucified with Christ," Paul said. "It is no longer I who live, but it is Christ

A Personal Commitment
to Christ

Dave

A friend of mine who had been raised as a Jehovah's Witness had become a Christian. One day he asked me to come over to his house, and as we visited he simply shared about how his life had radically changed. Even his face looked different. He was peaceful and he was joyful in a way I had never before seen him. He explained that he had made a personal commitment to Christ. In order to live as a Christian, he had turned from living life on his own. He said he believed that Jesus is the Son of God and had put him at the center of his life. I was nineteen at the time, and I was trying to get free of a lot of the things I was involved with that I knew were not good. I had never heard anybody talk about the fact that you could have a relationship with God through Christ. My friend's testimony had a life-changing impact on me. His experience prompted me to make a personal commitment to Christ, a decision that has oriented my whole life.

Faith is first and foremost a personal, intimate encounter with Jesus; it is having an experience of his closeness, his friendship and his love. It is in this way that we learn to know him ever better, to love him and to follow him more and more. May this happen to each one of us!

— Pope Benedict XVI, General audience, October 21, 2009

who lives in me. And the life I now live in the flesh I live by faith in the Son of God, who loved me and gave himself for me" (Galatians 2:20). Paul's encounter with Jesus redirected his life, which he spent continuing Christ's rescue mission.

Who Is Jesus Christ to You?

Jesus wants each of us to weigh his claim to be God. He asks us to respond to the question he once posed to the apostles: "Who do you say that I am?" At the beginning of this chapter I suggested that you consider this question. How have you or will you answer it, the most important question you will ever face?

Given what Jesus said about himself and all that he did, you confront an either/or situation. Jesus is either God or a lunatic, or worse. Who do *you* say that he is?

Jesus' Invitation

Like Paul, most of us are well aware of our wrongdoing. We bear traces of humanity's brokenness. We may feel guilty. We may be plagued by worry, depression, and fear. We may suffer from financial distress,

Liar, Lunatic, or Lord

I am trying here to prevent anyone from saying the really foolish thing people often say about him, "I'm ready to accept Jesus as a really great moral teacher, but I don't accept his claim to be God." That is the one thing that we must not say. A man who is merely a man, who said the sort of things Jesus said, would not be a great moral teacher. He would either be a lunatic, on the level with a man who says he is a poached egg, or else he would be the devil of hell. You must make your choice. Either this man was and is the Son of God or else a madman or something worse. You can shut him up for a fool, you can spit at him and kill him as a demon, or you can fall at his feet and call him Lord and God, but let us not come with any patronizing nonsense about his being a great human teacher. He has not left that open to us. He did not intend to.

— C. S. Lewis[6]

disease, addiction, joblessness, or damaged relationships. We may have had an abortion, viewed pornography habitually, or engaged in immoral behavior, either heterosexual or homosexual. We may feel that

> **"Those who love me will keep my word, and my Father will love them, and we will come to them and make our home with them."**
>
> — *John 14:23*

our life is going nowhere and that we are lost. Yet, like Paul and Dave, we have the opportunity to decide to commit our lives to Christ. We can choose to let him rescue us from all the evils that afflict us.

Jesus invites each of us to give our lives to him. He repeats to us his call to the first disciples: "Follow me!"

The Lord promises to come to all who seek him.

Chapter Three

What Does Jesus Want Us to Know?

Dave

What Did Jesus Come to Reveal?

You may have heard this story about a mother who was watching her four-year-old daughter draw a picture. "Maria, what are you drawing?" she asked. "I'm drawing a picture of God," said the child. The mother chuckled and said, "Honey, do you know that no one knows what God looks like?" The little girl looked up and said, "Mommy, in a moment you will."

True, no one has seen God, but that does not stop us from portraying him in our imaginations. For example, we may picture him as a kind old fellow with a white mane and flowing beard. Or we may depict him as a stern, black-robed judge, punishing us for every misstep. C. S. Lewis warns us about making such mental pictures of God because we may end up worshiping our imagined God instead of God as he really is.[7]

Jesus wants us to know God as he is. He came to reveal the nature of God to us. He declares in word and action that the eternal, infinite, all-powerful Creator of everything is our Father. He reveals him as a Father who loves us and wants to bring us into a personal relationship with him.

The New Testament presents Christianity as the divine family, with God welcoming us in Christ as his sons and daughters. The gospel of John, for example, says that Jesus gives to all believers the power to become children of the Father (see John 1:12). And St. Paul gives this wonderful snapshot of the Father's plan for us:

> **Blessed be the God and Father of our Lord
> Jesus Christ, who has blessed us in Christ
> with every spiritual blessing in the heavenly
> places, just as he chose us in Christ before
> the foundation of the world to be holy and
> blameless before him in love. He destined us for
> adoption as his children through Jesus Christ,
> according to the good pleasure of his will
> (Ephesians 1:3–6).**

God is our Father who loves us, cares for us, and relates to us personally. That's good news, but not immediately for everyone.

Look at Jesus to See the Father

Many people find it difficult to relate to God as Father because they have not had a good experience or memory of their own fathers. Some feel abandoned by their dads

> **The decline of fatherhood is one of the most basic, unexpected and extraordinary trends of our time.... Fifty percent of American children may be going to sleep each evening without being able to say good night to their dads.**
>
> — *David Popenoe*[8]

through death, divorce, or some other cause of a break in their relationship. Some have never known the father who fled at their birth or in their youth. Others have fathers who abused them physically or verbally. Some simply had fathers who were preoccupied with careers or problems and were not present to them. For many in these circumstances the mere mention of God as Father evokes anger, resentment, and mistrust. They tend to ignore the matter or deny the possibility of relating to him.

If you find yourself in this sad picture, I invite you to let Jesus introduce you to his Father and your Father. Reflecting on Jesus as he appears in Scripture and praying to the Holy Spirit can gently heal your woundedness. The Letter to the Hebrews says that Jesus "is the reflection of God's glory and the exact imprint of God's very being" (Hebrews 1:3). Jesus himself declared that

Finding My Father

Bert

My dad died when I was twelve years old, and as a teen I subconsciously set out on a "father hunt."… [A]t eighteen I became a friend of Professor William Storey, who took a real concern for me. Without my realizing it at the time, he became a spiritual father for me. Among his many gracious acts on my behalf, he taught me how to pray and live a dedicated Christian life.

Years later when I took stock of my "father hunt," I discovered that I had quietly entered a close relationship with my true Father, God himself. The realization struck me as I meditated on what it had meant for me to live in the Spirit. The Holy Spirit had arranged for me to become the Father's adopted son.

I had received the promise that St. Paul reported to the Ephesians: God "destined us for adoption as his children, through Jesus Christ" (Ephesians 1:5). What a wonderful gift it was to recognize that the Father loved me and wanted me as his child!

I now enjoy this father–son relationship with God. I thank him for it in my daily prayer, and I find myself trusting him a little more all the time.[9]

if you want to see the Father look at him. "If you know me," he said, "you will know my Father also…. Whoever has seen me has seen the Father" (John 14:7, 9).

At the risk of being irreverent, you might say in slang that Jesus is the spittin' image of his Father, as my sons are of me. For example, recently my son Jake appeared on a television series. Several of my friends from around the country called to tell me that they recognized him because he has my eyes and sounded just like me. Now, Jake does not resemble me exactly, but Jesus does bear the image of the Father perfectly.

Experiencing the Father's Love

Jesus shows us the Father so that we can experience God's love for us. He makes it impossible for us to believe that God is distant and that he doesn't care for us.

Consider with me the implications for our experience of God in this text from Paul's letter to the Galatians:

> **When the fullness of time had come, God sent his Son, born of a woman … to redeem those who were under the law, so that we might receive adoption as children. And because you are children, God has sent the Spirit of his Son into our hearts, crying, "Abba! Father!" So you are no longer a slave, but a child, and if a child then also an heir, through God (Galatians 4:4–7).**

Notice God's personal touch that appears throughout the passage.

- *"God sent his Son"* — The Father takes the initiative to send Jesus to us. He comes bringing God's love and mercy to each of us.

- *"to redeem those under the law"* — God sent Jesus to rescue us from sin, sickness, death, and the galaxy of all our troubles. "Redeem" means to save someone at a cost. God became a man in Christ so that he could suffer and die for us so that in Christ he could give us life. Bert's associate pastor, Monsignor Ed Thompson, at least once a week says that God would have done it even if you or I were the only person on the earth.

- *"so that we might receive adoption"* — God loved us so much that he adopted us as his children. He sent Jesus to bring you and me into his divine family as his sons and daughters. C. S. Lewis suspected that God created the whole universe just to have this lovely earth where he could enjoy a personal relationship with us.

- *"God sent the Spirit of his Son into our hearts, crying, 'Abba, Father.'"* — God gives us the Holy Spirit, who seals our relationship to him as daughters and sons. And he loves you and me so intimately that he wants us to call him "Abba," the affectionate Hebrew equivalent of "Dad" or "Papa."

- *"if a child then also an heir, through God"* — God arranges for us as sons and daughters to become co-heirs with Jesus, sharing in all the blessings of his relationship with the Father.

So, seeing Jesus dispels the false notion that the Father's love is a theoretical proposition, an answer to a question in a catechism, and not a personal reality.

What Does the Father's Love Look Like?

Scripture shows us the characteristics of God's love. The gospels, for example, give us a picture of the Father's care for us in the teaching and actions of Jesus. Consider, for example, Luke's account of Jesus' encounter with Zacchaeus, a tax collector (see Luke 19:1–10).

When I first read the New Testament as a teen, I was struck by the way Jesus associated with people on the fringes of Jewish society. He visited with tax collectors and dined with prostitutes and others that the Jewish leaders shunned. This sets the stage for the Zacchaeus story. He ranked lowest on the popularity index, hated by all from whom he collected taxes and enriched himself.

We catch up with Jesus as he enters the city of Jericho. A huge crowd crams the streets. Hundreds are following him, attracted by his teaching that stabs their hearts and his miracles that bring them hope. Buried somewhere in the throng is Zacchaeus, who burns with a desire to see Jesus. But he cannot catch sight of him because he is height-challenged. Imagine Danny Devito playing him in a movie. So he climbed a tree from which he hoped he would get a glimpse of Jesus as he passed by.

To Zacchaeus' surprise, Jesus stops under the tree, looks up at him, and says, "Hurry down, Zacchaeus. I want to spend the day with you at your house." That greeting must have caused the noisy crowd to go silent. They were stunned that Jesus would visit a man they hated as a robber. Someone grumbled, "What's this? The great holy man going off to the house of the town's biggest sinner!"

> **God's love was revealed among us in this way: God sent his only Son into the world so that we might live through him. In this is love, not that we loved God but that he loved us and sent his Son to be the atoning sacrifice for our sins.**
>
> *— 1 John 4:9–10*

Zacchaeus scurried down the tree as fast as he could. Something extraordinary happened to him before he hit the ground. For when he welcomed Jesus, he said, "Lord, I'm going to give half of my possessions to the poor. And if I have cheated anyone of anything I will pay them back four times as much." "That's exactly why I came," Jesus said, "to assure you that you are on the path to salvation." Scripture does not report this, but I think Jesus grasped Zacchaeus in a warm embrace.

In his meeting with Zacchaeus, Jesus manifested four defining characteristics of the Father's love:

- *The Father loves us first.* Just as Jesus initiated the conversation with Zacchaeus, God takes the initiative in loving us.

- *God's love for us is a gift.* Jesus feely decided to spend the day with Zacchaeus. His visit was a gift. God's love for us is his gift. It is not based on what we have done, good or bad, or what we have not done.

- *The Father loves each of us personally.* Jesus engaged Zacchaeus by stopping under the tree and calling him by name. Similarly, God expresses his love for us by engaging us in a personal relationship.

- *God loves us without cost or condition.* Jesus placed no conditions on his love for Zacchaeus. The Father loves us in the same way.

This story invites us to respond to God's love as Zacchaeus did. The Lord calls us by name just as he called Zacchaeus. He says he wants to come with his Father and make his home in us. Someone nearby may grumble, "What's this? How can the Father make a home in that sinner?" But God loves us freely. He wants to come to us no matter what we have done or failed to do. Nothing we ever do can change God's love for us. Nothing. All we must do is respond to his initiatives with a change of heart and mind ... just as Zacchaeus did.

Chapter Four

Why Do I Need a Savior?

Bert

There's Good News ...

If I were challenged to sum up God's message in Scripture in one sentence, I wouldn't hesitate to choose the following verse: "For God so loved the world that he gave his only Son, so that everyone who believes in him may not perish but may have eternal life" (John 3:16). This line — perhaps the most famously quoted text of the Bible — says it all. From Genesis to Revelation, every page of Scripture declares, "God loves you!"

Meditating on the following realities fills me with joy. The infinite, eternal, unchanging, all-powerful God:

- loved us before he created the universe;

- delights in us and wants us to know him;

- desires to draw us into a personal relationship.

He sent his only Son to become a man to show that he holds nothing back in his love for us. And Jesus spent himself to bring us into God's family.

That's good news.

... *And There's Bad News*

John 3:16 says God sent his Son "so that everyone who believes in him might not perish." The text suggests that evil circumstances threaten us and that God intends to save us from them. Do I need to persuade you that humanity needs a rescue operation? Just look at the bad news that the media report daily. Every year millions of people die from disease, famine, war, and natural disasters. Millions more suffer from poverty, crime, slavery, and injustice. Humanity seems to be in constant peril.

There's bad news on the personal level, too. Divorce bursts families, selfishness ruins friendships, and greed puts business associates at odds. We all feel the coldness and alienation that come from broken relationships. Many are in bondage to alcohol, drugs, or eating disorders. They struggle for freedom, but often lose hope. Others afflicted with depression or a mental illness despair of ever finding a way out. Sometimes people just feel lost because their lives have not worked out the way they wanted.

When we survey this scene, we feel that things are just not the way they're supposed to be. And they're not. Somehow humankind has slid off track.

Back to the Beginnings

To figure out what has gone wrong with humanity, we must go back to our beginnings. We can learn about them in Genesis, the first book of the Bible. Chapters one through three of that book reveal important truths about the origins of humankind. Genesis does not claim to present scientific evidences. So we can set aside contemporary issues over evolution and creationism and consider the biblical message.

> **God saw everything that he had made, and indeed, it was very good.**
>
> *— Genesis 1:31*

The first chapter of Genesis describes God's creative activity. He made light, sky, earth and sea, plants and trees, fish and birds, animals, and finally men and women. God declared each creation good. After he created human beings, he declared everything he had made "very good." He meant especially women and men, you and me, the zenith of his creation.

Genesis also teaches that God created men and women in his own image. He designed us to be like him so that he could bring us into a relationship with him. As we have seen in Chapter Three, God wanted human beings to be daughters and sons in his divine family. To make this possible, he instilled in us certain of his characteristics, such as the capacities for knowing and loving. Prominently among these qualities, God gave us free will. He did not want robots that he could program

> What Satan put into the heads of our remote ancestors was the idea that they could "be like gods" — could set up on their own as if they had created themselves — be their own masters — invent some sort of happiness for themselves outside God, apart from God. And out of that hopeless attempt has come nearly all that we call human history — money, poverty, ambition, war, prostitution, classes, empires, slavery — the long terrible story of man trying to find something other than God which will make him happy.
>
> — *C. S. Lewis*[10]

to do things to please him. He wanted children who would freely choose to love and obey him. Because God loved us so much, he was willing to take the risk that we might freely choose to reject him. That's what we did, to our great cost and God's as well.

What Went Wrong?

The third chapter of Genesis describes an event that had catastrophic effects we still experience. The devil persuaded Adam and Eve that they could become like God if they disobeyed him. Mesmerized by the temptation, our first parents turned away from God. They decided that they could not count on him to provide all that they needed for happiness. So they thought they would become like God and do it themselves.

We call this tragic event the original sin. From the first couple this sin has spread through the ages to all humanity, infecting us with a full spectrum of evil inclinations. We recognize its traces in our warped behavior.

I'll Do It Myself

Bert

Shortly after I enrolled at Notre Dame in Fall 1963, I connected with an informal community of students and faculty who were engaged in evangelization. For a year I split my time between studying and doing what I believed was the Lord's work on the campus. In Spring 1964 I married Mary Lou Cuddyre, my high school sweetheart, who shared my Christian commitment and experience. To my surprise, a year later I flunked my master's exam, a disastrous first for me, who had always been an "A" student. I raged at God because I thought he should have helped me since I thought I had been helping him. So I decided to do it myself and show off by skipping the master's exam and passing the Ph.D. exam a year later. I stopped praying and abandoned all my campus Christian activities. As a result, I plunged into a severe depression. I made life miserable for Mary Lou (just ask her). But she and my friends kept praying for me and reaching out to me until I gradually emerged from my funk in Summer 1966. I started to pray again and resumed my involvements with my colleagues. And finally accepting God's grace, I passed the doctoral exam.[12]

"Original sin," said G. K. Chesterton, "is the only part of Christian theology which can really be proved."[11] We prove it by sinning multiple times every day.

Sin promises that we can make ourselves happy. Instead, when we sin we make ourselves miserable. For example, I experienced a severe depression when I turned from God because of a failure in graduate school (see sidebar on page 51). When we try to fix our brokenness, we fail because we cannot do it on our own. We were created for friendship with God, which is the source of happiness. Sin breaks our relationship with him. St. Paul says, "The wages of sin is death" (Romans 6:23). He's not talking about mere physical death, but the spiritual death of separation from God.

God's Remedy

No matter how hard we may try, we cannot fix the breach with God on our own. Our attempting to be good falls far short of repairing the damage sin has done to us. We need God's help. He always planned to rescue us and restore our friendship with him. The wages of sin may be death, but St. Paul assures us that "the free gift of God is eternal life in Christ Jesus" (Romans 6:23).

When Jesus first appeared on the scene, St. John the Baptist, his forerunner,

> **God's love was revealed among us in this way: God sent his only Son into the world so that we might live through him. In this is love, not that we loved God but that he loved us and sent his Son to be the atoning sacrifice for our sins.**
>
> *— 1 John 4:9–10*

No "Self-Help" for Sin

Paul's proclamation that Christ died for our sins draws a line across our lives. The message challenges us to look inside and ask questions like, "Why am I bent toward bad behaviors?" and "Why do twisted thoughts ramble through my mind?" We know deep down that we cannot fix such things ourselves. We need a savior. Our spouse, our best friend, our therapist, our priest, or anyone else cannot rescue us. The Savior is God himself who came to us in his Son, who loved us and gave himself for us (see Galatians 2:20).

pointed him out to his followers: "Here is the Lamb of God who takes away the sin of the world!" (John 1:29). John was announcing that God had taken the initiative and sent his Son to deal with our sins. He embraced death so that in Christ he could give us the gift of eternal life and heal the breach in our relationship with him.

Twenty years after the death and Resurrection of Christ, St. Paul was still repeating this astounding statement: "I handed on to you as of *first importance* what I in turn had received: that Christ died for our sins ... that he was buried, and that he was raised on the third day" (1 Corinthians 15:3–4, emphasis added). That Christ gathered up in his flesh every sin — past, present, and future — and obliterated them on the cross — was the substance of Paul's message. Nothing was more important for him, and nothing is more important for us than to realize that Christ died to set us free from our sins.

Our Response

Fifty days after Jesus' Resurrection, thousands of people in Jerusalem witnessed the dramatic outpouring of the Holy Spirit on his disciples. Peter addressed their wonderment by preaching the first sermon in the history of the church (Acts 2:14–40). He explained that they were witnessing the fulfillment of Old Testament prophecies that their leaders had brought about by condemning Jesus to death. They had handed him over to be crucified, but God had raised him from the dead.

> **There is a God-shaped vacuum in the heart of every man which cannot be filled by any created thing, but only by God, the Creator, made known through Jesus.**
>
> *— Blaise Pascal*

And he had sent the Holy Spirit that caused the marvelous tumult they observed.

Struck by grace, the crowd cried out, "What must we do?" Peter said, "Repent, and be baptized every one of you in the name of Jesus Christ so that your sins may be forgiven; and you will receive the gift of the Holy Spirit" (Acts 2:38). That was the bottom-line response for Peter's hearers. And repentance and baptism is our response to the Good News as well.

Repent and be baptized — what do these responses involve? Let's take them in reverse order. Baptism gives us the Holy Spirit who brings us into God's fami-

Just Pray to Jesus

Dave

My friend's testimony about his conversion turned my life around (see "A Personal Commitment to Christ" on page 33). Over several months my desire to know Jesus grew more and more intense. One day I went to his house and told him I wanted to pray. He said, "Pray to Jesus out loud." I was used to saying the prayers we say at Mass and the Our Father, but he was telling me to pray in my own words. So I simply prayed, "Jesus, help me." And God was so merciful. In my turning to him, he came to me. I experienced a renewal of the Holy Spirit that I received at my baptism.

ly as his children and makes us members of the Body of Christ, the church. Many of us were baptized as infants, some as adults. Others who are not baptized and want to become Christians may inquire about how to proceed at a local Catholic parish.

Repentance means having a change of heart and mind. It is an appropriate response to the gospel for both the unbaptized and the baptized. For persons seeking baptism, repentance expresses their desire to commit themselves to Christ and come to know him.

For baptized Christians, it affirms their commitment to the Lord and declares their desire to know him more personally.

The act of repentance involves facing up to our sins and admitting our need for a savior. Just as Dave did many years ago, it means giving our lives to Christ (see sidebar on page 55). We acknowledge our sins, express faith in Jesus, and invite him into our lives. Christ does the rest. He comes into our hearts. He makes himself known to us. He fills us with the Holy Spirit.

In this wonderful exchange, we have nothing to lose, and everything to gain. I invite you to close this book now and respond to the Lord in your own words. Do what Dave's friend told him to do: pray to Jesus out loud.

> **If you confess with your lips that Jesus is Lord and believe in your heart that God raised him from the dead, you will be saved.**
>
> *— Romans 10:9*

Chapter Five

Why Is the Resurrection Important for Us?

Dave

The New Testament Evidence

Around A.D. 56, St. Paul wrote his first letter to the Christian community at Corinth. In it he made the following noteworthy statement about people who had met Jesus after he had died and had risen from the dead:

> **For I handed on to you as of first importance what I in turn had received: that Christ died for our sins in accordance with the scriptures, and that he was buried, and that he was raised on the third day in accordance with the scriptures, and that he appeared to Cephas, then to the twelve. Then he appeared to more than five hundred brothers and sisters at one**

time, most of whom are still alive, though some have died. Then he appeared to James, then to all the apostles (1 Corinthians 15:3–7).

Scholars who are experienced judges of evidence regard this as a persuasive testimony to the Resurrection. In this very early document written less than a quarter century after the event, Paul listed eyewitnesses to whom Jesus had appeared. Among these were James, Peter (Cephas), and the other apostles. Remarkably, Paul also reported that Jesus appeared to 500 men and women at one time. He noted that most of them were still alive — a clear invitation to doubters to seek them out, interview them, and check out their stories. Paul's appeal to these numerous witnesses makes his account very credible.

The Resurrection is the core reality and the central tenet of the Christian faith. Christians believe that Christ's rising from the dead overcame sin and death. We see it as the ultimate expression of God's love that transformed ev-

> If there is no resurrection of the dead, then Christ has not been raised; and if Christ has not been raised, then our proclamation has been in vain and your faith has been in vain.... If Christ has not been raised, your faith is futile and you are still in your sins. Then those who have died in Christ have perished. If for this life only we have hoped in Christ, we are of all people most to be pitied.
>
> — 1 Corinthians 15:13–14, 17–19

erything from our individual lives to the cosmos itself. St. Paul says that if Christ did not arise, Christians are deluded, locked in their sins, and doomed (see 1 Corinthians 15:12–19).

But Christ was raised from the dead, and Scripture gives convincing evidence for the fact.

In the first place, the New Testament demonstrates that Jesus' crucifixion and Resurrection occurred as the deliberate plan of God for the salvation of humankind. All the gospels show Jesus telling that he must suffer, die, be buried, and raised after three days (see Matthew 16:21, Mark 8:31, Luke 9:22, and John 12:27). But his closest associates neither believed nor even understood what he was saying. For example, Matthew described Peter's inspired response to Jesus' question, "Who do you say that I am?" The chief of the apostles answered, "You are the Messiah, the Son of the Living God" (Matthew 16:15–16). After praising Peter and establishing him as the head of the church he was building, Jesus began announcing his coming death:

> **From that time on, Jesus began to show his disciples that he must go to Jerusalem and undergo great suffering at the hands of the elders and chief priests and scribes, and be killed, and on the third day be raised. And Peter took him aside and began to rebuke him, saying, "God forbid it, Lord! This must never happen to you" (Matthew 16:21–22).**

The apostles expected the Messiah to deliver Israel from the oppression of Rome. Jesus' talk about suffering and death made no sense to them if he was supposed to wage war against the Romans. They just didn't get it that he was going to conquer at a deeper level the forces of evil that dominated humankind. The apostles' lack of understanding stands as evidence against the notion that they fabricated the account of the Resurrection to cover up the fact of Jesus' death. As the gospels show, they never saw it coming. Had they been inventing the story they would not have presented themselves as clueless.

The despair of Jesus' closest associates at his death further demonstrates this point. None of the disciples expected Jesus to be raised from the dead. For example, consider Mary Magdalene and other women of Galilee, who had watched the crucifixion from a distance (see Luke 23:54–24:11). Jesus was taken down from the cross and laid in a tomb just before the Sabbath had begun. The women wanted to anoint his corpse with spices and ointments, but had to obey the Sabbath rest.

They went to the tomb early on the first day of the week to perform this kindness, but were perplexed when they did not find the body. Instead, two men in dazzling clothes told them that Jesus had risen and reminded them that he had predicted his death and Resurrection. Terrified at first, then astounded with the news, the women ran to tell the apostles that Jesus had risen. Luke recorded their reaction: "But these words seemed to them an idle tale, and they did not believe them" (Luke 24:11). Drained of all hope, they could not fathom that Jesus had risen. If the apostles were making up the story, it is unimaginable that they would have reported their blatant unbelief.

Significant also is the fact that the gospels present women as the first witnesses to Jesus' Resurrection. At that time, Jewish women had no social status and could not testify in court. Their word just did not count. If Jesus' followers were fabricating the Resurrection account, they would not have made women the first witnesses to the Resurrection. That fact enhances the authenticity of the New Testament testimony.

The Proclamation of the Apostles

Further scriptural evidence for the Resurrection comes from the message that the disciples chose to proclaim. When they addressed the crowds, they did not lead with Jesus' teachings. They could have taught lessons from his Sermon on the Mount (Matthew 5–7) or from his discourse at the Last Supper (John 14–16), but they didn't. They didn't recount the miracles that he performed. Instead, they advanced a simple and provocative message: Christ was raised from the dead. As they proclaimed Jesus' Resurrection, signs and wonders occurred and many came to faith.

For example, one day Peter and John were going to the temple to pray (see Acts 3). A beggar who was lame from birth asked them for alms. Peter explained that he had no money but he would give him what he had. Calling upon the power of the Resurrection, he said, "In the name of Jesus Christ of Nazareth, stand up and walk" (Acts 3:6). Instantly healed, the beggar jumped up and began "walking and leaping and praising God" (Acts 3:8).

The bystanders were amazed. They gathered around the apostles, wondering what had happened. Peter told the crowd to stop staring at them, as though they had healed the man by their own power or holiness. He explained that out of ignorance they and their rulers had handed Jesus over to be crucified. Then Peter said: "You killed the Author of life, whom God raised from the dead. To this we are witnesses. And by faith in his name, his name itself has made this man strong, whom you see and know; and the faith that is through Jesus has given him this perfect health in the presence of all of you" (Acts 3:15–16).

About five thousand men who heard Peter believed. Trying to stop the groundswell, Jewish leaders, including some Sadducees, who did not believe in resurrection, arrested Peter and John. The next day Peter, with the healed beggar alongside him, made this defense before a council of high priests and elders: "Let it be known to all of you, and to all the people of Israel, that this man is standing before you in good health by the name of Jesus Christ of Nazareth, whom you crucified, whom God raised from the dead" (Acts 4:10). Nothing fancy, no eloquent rationale … just a simple declaration of the fact of the Resurrection.

The council was stymied. They recognized that something marvelous had happened through these men. They wanted to curb their growing influence over the people. All that the leaders had to do to refute the apostles' testimony was produce the body of Jesus. They could have used their connections with the Roman authorities to have it brought forward. But Jesus' body was not available because he had been raised. So the leaders did the only thing they could. They forbade the apostles to speak or teach in the name of Jesus. Peter and John stood their ground. They said, "Whether it is right in God's sight to listen to you rather than to God, you must judge; for we cannot keep from speaking about what we have seen and heard" (Acts 4:19–20).

These followers of Jesus were simple, uneducated men. They were not weaving some complicated fiction to cover up the death of Jesus and to hide their grief. They were full of joy because they had become witnesses of his Resurrection. And they could not keep themselves from declaring it.

Why Is the Resurrection Important for Us?

The Resurrection of Jesus has vast implications for you and me. It is not an event locked in the past, buried in the pages of a dust-covered history book. The Resurrection has consequences for you and me right now. That's why Christians declare, "Christ *is* risen," rather than, "Christ *was* risen."

The Resurrection assures us of the truth of Christianity because it validates all that Jesus claimed and taught. That the Father raised him from death irrefutably demonstrates that he is the Son of God. Christ's rising appeals to our minds. It demands our assent and becomes the ground of our faith.

When Jesus rose, he destroyed death for all of us. He fulfilled his promise that "I am the resurrection and

The "Why" of the Resurrection

It was necessary for Christ to suffer and to rise again from the dead:

- for our instruction in the faith, since our belief in Christ's divinity is confirmed by His being raised from the dead;

- for the raising of our hope, since through seeing Christ, who is our Lord, being raised from the dead, we hope that we likewise shall be raised;

- to set in order the lives of the faithful: according to Romans 6:4: "As Christ was raised from the dead by the glory of the Father, so we too might walk in newness of life";

- in order to complete the work of our salvation: because, just as for this reason did He endure evil things in dying that He might deliver us from evil, so was He glorified in having been raised from death in order to advance us toward good things.

St. Thomas Aquinas[13]

the life. Those who believe in me, even though they die, will live, and everyone who lives and believes in me will never die" (John 11:25-26). The Resurrection puts to rest all our fears that we would be obliterated when we die. It assures us of the grace of immortality. The Lord will raise us up and transform our risen bodies, making them imperishable just like his resurrected body.

We don't have to wait for our death and resurrection to enjoy our new life in Christ. Jesus was talking about you and me when he said, "I came that they may have life, and have it abundantly" (John 10:10). At baptism we receive a share in Christ's resurrected life. The Holy Spirit comes to us and makes us daughters and sons of God who begin right away to live a new life in Christ. St. Paul says, "If anyone is in Christ, there is a new creation: everything old has passed away; see, everything has become new!" (2 Corinthians 5:17).

> **When this perishable body puts on imperishability, and this mortal body puts on immortality, then the saying that is written will be fulfilled:**
>
> **"Death has been swallowed up in victory."**
> **"Where, O death, is your victory?**
> **Where, O death, is your sting?"**
>
> — *1 Corinthians 15:54–55*

The splendid experience of eternal life, our vibrant sharing in Christ's Resurrection, is only a word away. Jesus stands before us bursting with desire to fill us with his new life. All we must do to receive it is to ask him for it.

Chapter Six

Who Is the Holy Spirit?

Dave

The Love of God

Catholics and other Christians believe that God is a Trinity — three persons in one divine nature. We could never have discovered this truth on our own. Our reason could not have figured it out. God himself had to reveal his "threeness," which he gradually unfolded to us in Scripture. In the New Testament Jesus gave us the full picture. For example, in John's gospel he spoke plainly about three persons in God. To Jewish leaders who doubted him, he declared, "The Father and I are one" (John 10:30). And

> **The notion of one God who is three persons must be profoundly mysterious. We could not know it at all if God had not drawn the veil aside that we might see.**
>
> — *F. J. Sheed*[14]

in his farewell address at the Last Supper, Jesus promised the disciples that they would receive the Holy Spirit: "The Holy Spirit, whom the Father will send in my name, will teach you everything" (John 14:26).

When Jesus spoke to his disciples about the Holy Spirit, he was not presenting an interesting theory about God. He was pledging that they would receive the Spirit with such life-changing power that they would never be the same. Just before Jesus ascended to heaven, he directed his disciples to wait expectantly for the promised Holy Spirit. He said, "You will receive power when the Holy Spirit has come upon you; and you will be my witnesses in Jerusalem, in all Judea and Samaria, and to the ends of the earth" (Acts 1:8).

That's what happened ten days later. The Holy Spirit came with extraordinary signs upon a hundred and twenty disciples, including Jesus' mother Mary. A loud wind and tongues of fire announced his presence. All experienced the Spirit's profound touch and began to praise God in unlearned languages. The event caused such a commotion that thousands of visitors to Jerusalem ran to the scene, wondering what

The event caused such a commotion that thousands of visitors to Jerusalem ran to the scene, wondering what was going on.

was going on. Peter addressed the crowd, explaining that Jesus was raised from the dead and, now in heaven, had poured out the promised Holy Spirit.

I want to say more about this event later, but for now notice that the receiving of the Spirit was undeniably experiential. No one could doubt that something significant, even something wonderful, had happened to the disciples. As Jesus promised, God had released a power that changed their lives. Peter provided striking evidence for the Spirit's transforming grace. The man who had fearfully denied Jesus fifty days earlier now fearlessly testified to his resurrection before some who may have arranged for his crucifixion.

The Holy Spirit descended upon the disciples nearly 2,000 years ago. They didn't have to believe that he would empower them. They had experienced his love and could give examples of what he had done for them. Today, twenty centuries later, the Spirit still lets us experience the transforming power of his love. One answer to the question posed in the title of this chapter is that the Holy Spirit is the person of the Trinity who reveals God's love to us. He lets us know deep within and irrefutably that God cares for us, delights in us, and wants the best for us.

> **God's love has been poured into our hearts through the Holy Spirit that has been given to us.**
>
> — *Romans 5:5*

Once I was praying for a renewal in the Spirit with a group of people in London, England. I noticed that Martin, an Irish soccer player, had slipped off to a corner. I went to see if he was alright and found him weeping uncontrollably. "Martin, are you okay?" I asked. He was sobbing so hard that he could barely talk. Through his tears, he blubbered, "He … He … He called me 'son.'" Through the Holy Spirit, Martin had experienced the Father's love. We can expect the Spirit to do the same for us.

Transformed by Love

(The priest in this story was nicknamed Fr. Paul because, like St. Paul, he had a dramatic conversion.)

Fr. Paul, a priest in an African country, began having a difficult time two years after his ordination. He began to drink heavily. He also violated his commitment to celibacy numerous times. Fr. Paul decided that it just wasn't going to work and that he no longer wanted to be a priest. He thought he might pursue a career in politics. So he looked for opportunities to develop relationships. Fr. Paul learned that some movers and shakers from his country were scheduled to attend a Catholic retreat at a nearby center. Thinking that he might network with important people, he decided to attend the event.

During the first session, a young man gave a talk about the basics of the Christian faith. At first Fr. Paul listened attentively, but at a certain point he lost track of the talk and began to experience an increasing sense of the Lord's presence. He said later that he realized that the Lord Jesus seemed to be coming toward him. And the closer he drew to Fr. Paul, the more Fr. Paul trembled.

He was so touched by the love of Christ for him that he felt convicted of all his wrongdoing. He fell down, and lying on his back, he interrupted the speaker by loudly confessing his sins for all to hear.

Then Fr. Paul experienced the Holy Spirit cleansing him, bringing him forgiveness, and flooding him with love. He said, "I lifted my hands up and started thanking God because I knew he had come to me and had mercy on me." He sensed God was commissioning him for service. He heard the Lord say, "I called you to be a priest and have anointed you to preach the gospel to the poor. I'm giving you a second chance." Soon Fr. Paul launched a spiritual revival in his country that touched the lives of many people.[15]

Changed from the Inside Out

God the Father sends the Holy Spirit to all who believe in his Son. He wants us to have a firsthand experience of his love. The gift of the Spirit brings us a new life that changes us from the inside out. His presence frees us from the sins that have tied us up in knots.

We can see in Scripture the gradual unfolding of the Father's plan to pour out the Holy Spirit on all humankind. In the Old Testament, a few individuals designated for some specific service received the Spirit. For example, the Spirit rushed on King David for his leadership of the people and he inspired the prophets who spoke for God (see 1 Samuel 16:13). But many centuries before the coming of Christ, God revealed his marvelous intentions for humanity. He announced that he would enter a new relationship with us and that he would give us his Spirit, who would transform us from within. For example, through Ezekiel he made this promise: "A new heart I will give you, and a new spirit I will put within you;... I will put my spirit within you, and make you follow my statutes and be careful to observe my ordinances" (Ezekiel 36:26–27).

By his death and Resurrection, Jesus made this new life available to us. The Holy Spirit will flood our hearts with love and release us to live with freedom and joy. We can have this internal makeover for the asking, yet many Catholics burden themselves with an inadequate idea of the Christian life. We have the misconception that being Christian means doing good things.

For instance, I once held this mistaken view. At 19, I felt that I should decide to become a faithful Catholic. Since I thought being Christian meant being good, I decided that I had to get my act together before I could make a commitment to be a better Catholic. I tried very hard to get the junk out of my life, but I couldn't do it. It was like dragging bags of trash from a house that always burst before I reached the door. I could not change my life. I had to come to grasp the good news that God out of his love for me sends the Holy Spirit to change me from the inside out.

Ready for Action

The Holy Spirit ... apportions grace to each person as he wills. Like a dry tree that puts forth shoots when watered, the soul bears the fruit of holiness when repentance has made it worthy of receiving the Holy Spirit. Although the Spirit never changes, the effects of his action, by the will of God and in the name of Christ, are both many and marvelous.

The Spirit makes one person a teacher of divine truth, inspires another to prophecy, gives another the power of casting out devils, enables another to interpret holy Scripture. The spirit strengthens one person's self-control, shows another how to help the poor.... His action is different in different people, but the Spirit himself is always the same.

— *St. Cyril of Jerusalem*[16]

Equipped for Service

In addition to providing the grace for our personal transformation, the Holy Spirit plays an important role in advancing the work of Christ. The Spirit empowers us to participate in the rescue mission that Jesus launched when he proclaimed God's kingdom. Our spiritual renewal equips us to join with him to communicate the good news to others in both word and action.

At baptism every Christian receives gifts that equip him to join in the work of bringing others to Christ and the church. The Spirit imparts a great variety of gifts, including teaching, healing, administration, and service. But all work together for the common good and for building up the body of Christ (see 1 Corinthians 12:7 and Ephesians 4:12).

For example, Bert says that the Holy Spirit has given him a gift of communication:

As a young man I recognized that I had a natural ability to explain things clearly. The Holy Spirit has shaped this skill into a gift that I can use in his service. I describe it as a capacity to encourage others with words. I have learned to use it in conducting one-on-one relationships, in giving talks, and in writing. I like to think that my exercising this gift helps to advance God's kingdom in some small way.[17]

Once I heard a successful businessman share that for many years he had felt he was born at the wrong time. He wished he had lived at some more significant period in history, such as the American Revolution. But after the Holy Spirit renewed his life, he realized that God was inviting him to join the greatest adventure of all. He was called to become a disciple of Christ and

to impact people in ways that have everlasting consequences.

Like this businessman, we must discover that life
is not about us. It's about God. He wants us to see that
we are part of a bigger story, the great and wonderful
story of salvation from sin, sickness, and death. Jesus,
the Hero of God's story, is moving events to a cosmic
climax. And he wants us to link our stories with his so
that we can contribute to the grand conclusion — eternal life with him.

Ratifying Faith

God intends that we live a joy-filled life in the Holy
Spirit. But many Christians do not seem to enjoy this
experience. That's because, unlike the earliest Christians, they have not made for themselves the commitments that engage God's promise of the Spirit.

In the first-century church, most people were converted to Christ as adults. At their baptism they committed their life to him.
They understood that par-
ticipation in the sacrament
meant their sharing in the
death and resurrection of
Jesus. When they were
immersed in the baptismal
pool, they died with Christ.
And when they climbed
out, they rose with him to
a new life. St. Paul had this
in mind when he wrote,

> **The declaration that Jesus
> is Lord is meant to be an
> expression of a person's
> commitment.... [W]e need a
> radical conversion that will
> make the presence of God
> real and personal for each
> one of us.**
>
> — *Peter Cardinal Turkson*[18]

> **Is it not true that nearly all Christians prove unfaithful to the promises made to Jesus in baptism? Where does this universal failure come from, if not from man's habitual forgetfulness of the promises and responsibilities of baptism and from the fact that scarcely anyone makes a personal ratification of the contract made with God through his sponsors?**
>
> — *St. Louis de Montfort*[19]

"We have been buried with him by baptism into death, so that, just as Christ was raised from the dead by the glory of the Father, we too might walk in newness of life" (Romans 6:4). The reception of the sacrament dramatically expressed their commitment to follow Christ and activated the power of the Holy Spirit. And it gave them the experience of the Spirit that empowered them to live a joyful and productive Christian life.

But today most Catholics receive the sacrament of baptism as infants. Our godparents stand in for us as sponsors. They profess our faith for us. Rarely do many Catholics deliberately ratify the commitments that godparents make on our behalf. If we want to receive the full life of the Spirit God promises, as adults we must confess our faith in Christ and the church.

Making an adult faith commitment to Christ and the church disposes us to experience a release of the Spirit. Then we must activate the graces of baptism by turning to the Lord and asking him to release the Holy Spirit in our lives. That's the topic of the next chapter.

Engaging Jesus

Bert

I am a cradle Catholic. I was raised by a faithful single-parent mother. She modeled basic Catholic piety for me and put me through Catholic schools. But my Christian life was somewhat superficial until I met some serious Catholic students and teachers at Duquesne University in Pittsburgh, Pennsylvania. They invited me to pray with them, which I did every morning for several years. Together we formed a group called Chi Rho that sponsored Bible studies and informal courses on Catholic topics. I caught faith from these friends. Their love for the Lord was contagious.

I remember occasions during my college years when I was especially aware of Christ's presence. At those times I engaged him in prayer. And although I don't remember the words I said, in these moments I committed myself to follow him. For instance, once at a Bible study I was deeply moved by John 14:23, where Jesus says that if I love him and obey him, he and his Father will love me and make their home in me. That promise stunned me. I wanted Jesus to come to me, and I invited him to do it. Fifty years later that text still stuns me. It comes to my mind often, and when it does I renew my commitment to follow Christ.

Chapter Seven

The Holy Spirit and You

Dave

Transformed by the Holy Spirit

I have already written briefly about my conversion and adult faith commitment. Now I want to tell my story more fully to show how the Holy Spirit works to transform our lives.

I grew up in the 1960s in a typical Catholic family. We went to Mass together every Sunday. My dad gave me the good example of kneeling to pray at bedtime and giving generously in the collections at church. He also sang loud at Mass, which used to bother me, but now I do the same.

At 13, I saw the Beatles on the Ed Sullivan Show and got hooked. I idolized them through my teen years. I played in rock bands, became a long-haired hippie, and embraced a dissolute lifestyle. For several years my life spiraled downward. Then, when I was 19, my friend Richard was converted to Christ and baptized in the Holy Spirit. As I shared in Chapter Two, his testimony of this experience turned me around.

Raised a Jehovah's Witness, Richard had also become a hippie as a youth, growing hair down to his waist and sporting a huge pirate earring. Then an elderly Christian man told the teen-aged Richard how he could have a whole new and happy life. All he had to do was turn to Jesus and engage in a relationship with him. Then he could have his sins forgiven and receive the fullness of the Holy Spirit. And Richard did it. He committed his life to Christ and by the power of the Spirit began to turn his life around.

> **Raised a Jehovah's Witness, Richard had also become a hippie as a youth, growing hair down to his waist and sporting a huge pirate earring.**

About the same time, I had become deeply dissatisfied with the way things were going for me. I was struggling to get my life together. And it wasn't happening. Contrasted with how my life was going I could see that Richard had actually changed! One day he explained what Christ and the Spirit had done for him and it intrigued me. But in the next few months my life fell apart. Looking back, it seems as though the Lord pulled the rug out from underneath my feet so that I would fall on my knees before him.

Finally, in desperation, I called Richard. I told him I would like to come to his place and pray with him. And he invited me over. When I arrived, he repeated what he had already told me about his relationship with Christ and the Holy Spirit. Then he said, "Kneel down, and pray out loud to Jesus in your own words." Richard could tell that I was unsure of what to do, so he said, "Just pray like you're talking to Jesus right here." He also explained that he would lay his hands on me as a way of praying that the Holy Spirit would come to me.

So from my gut I prayed, "Jesus, help me!" That's all I said, but that was enough. Two very significant things happened simultaneously. From deep within, I surrendered to Jesus, turning to him and away from my wasted lifestyle. And I experienced the presence of the Holy Spirit moving in me from head to toe. I was awestruck by the sense of God's love for me. "Lord," I said, "I never want to leave you again."

> **So from my gut I prayed, "Jesus, help me!" That's all I said, but that was enough.**

Later, I reflected on this event. I saw that I was now enjoying a personal relationship with the Lord, which I never knew was possible. I recognized that he had always been with me. Even when I was drinking and using drugs, he had protected me from danger and death. Without a doubt, the Holy Spirit had radically changed my life. John's Gospel declares that Jesus is the Lamb of God who takes away the sin of the world, and that includes my sins. The gospels also describe him as the baptizer in the Holy Spirit. He had done those pivotal things for me. He cleaned me up from my sins and released in me the power of the Spirit I had received at baptism.

Marks of Renewal in the Holy Spirit

Being baptized in the Spirit produces transforming effects in our lives. Some people, like me, experience a dramatic and sudden spiritual renewal. For others, the results of spiritual renewal occur gradually, but not less significantly. Here I want to describe some of the common things the Holy Spirit does for us and illustrate them with my experience.

> [John the Baptist] proclaimed, "The one who is more powerful than I is coming after me; I am not worthy to stoop down and untie the thong of his sandals. I have baptized you with water; but he will baptize you with the Holy Spirit."
>
> — *Mark 1:7–8*

Experiencing the love of God. The Holy Spirit makes the love of God come alive for us. God's plan has always been to bring us into his divine family, where he would love us as his daughters and sons (see John 1:12–13 and Ephesians 1:4–5). We receive God's love not by what we do, but by who we are. It's a matter not of performance, but of identity. Jesus said that he loves us with the same love that the Father has for him (see John 15:9). The day I prayed with Richard I sensed the Spirit flooding me with the love of God. I became absolutely convinced that the Father loved me, and that conviction has never left me.

Realizing the forgiveness of sins. As I have already shared, when I was baptized in the Spirit, I experienced the Lord cleansing me of all my sins. Jesus, the God-man, came among us just so that he could destroy our sins on the cross (see Romans 5:8–9). The Holy Spirit brings that truth home to us with unforgettable joy. With the psalmist we can celebrate that "as far as the east is from the west, so far [the Lord] removes our transgressions from us" (Psalm 103:12).

Receiving power for Christian living. Jesus promised that we would receive power when we were baptized in the Holy Spirit (see Acts 1:8). He meant that we

> My prayers, which had mostly been formal, now became personal and intimate because I was experiencing God's presence.

would be empowered both for sharing the good news and also for daily Christian living (see Romans 5:10). The Lord has faithfully enlivened me beginning the night I received a release of the Spirit.

Desiring prayer, Scripture, and the sacraments. Shortly after I was baptized in the Spirit, I noticed strong desires to pray, to read Scripture, and to receive the sacraments. Renewal in the Spirit commonly draws people to respond to God with these essential Christian resources. I began to pray and reflect on Scripture daily. And I received the Eucharist and went to confession frequently.

My prayers, which had mostly been formal, now became personal and intimate because I was experiencing God's presence. The words of Scripture jumped off the page for me. They became life-giving, relevant, and important for my relationship with Jesus. And I realized that I was encountering him when I received the

Eucharist and when I confessed my sins to him at Reconciliation.

Praising and thanking God. People who are baptized in the Holy Spirit commonly find themselves wanting to praise and thank God. That's what happened to me. I had some limited experience of these forms of prayer. But after my renewal in the Spirit, praise and thanksgiving seemed to flow from me. These expressions of worship well up in us because commitment to Christ and a release of the Spirit put us in a right relationship with God.

> "I am the vine, you are the branches. Those who abide in me and I in them bear much fruit because apart from me you can do nothing."
>
> — *John 15:5*

Growing in Christian character. St. Paul says that the Holy Spirit enables us to replace bad behaviors like fighting, anger, and lust with good behaviors like peacemaking, patience, and self-control. He calls these character traits "the fruit of the Spirit" (see Galatians 5:22). Jesus himself taught that we would produce good fruit in our lives if we stayed close to him (see John 15:5).

Bert says that he senses the Holy Spirit helping him to be faithful to his daily prayer time, to relate to his wife and family with kindness, and to serve elderly and sick neighbors with compassion. And for me, in the years after I received the Spirit, he changed my character, enabling me to shed my longtime bad behaviors and learn new good ones.

Developing community relationships. The Holy Spirit makes us realize that we are the family of God and that we need the support of brothers and sisters. In my case, after I was baptized in the Spirit I had to break with my anti-Christian friends. They thought I was nuts, felt betrayed, and tried to drag me back to a sinful lifestyle. I formed new friendships with other young men and women who were living as Spirit-led Christians. We got together for a Bible study and social activities. Gradually we developed more serious relationships. We committed ourselves to pray for each other and support each other in whatever ways were needed. We also reached out to others to share the wonderful life that we had found in Jesus Christ. We came to enjoy the kind of community life that the Lord and the church want for all believers.

> We have gifts that differ according to the grace given to us: prophecy, in proportion to faith; ministry, in ministering; the teacher, in teaching; the exhorter, in exhortation; the giver in generosity; the leader, in diligence; the compassionate, in cheerfulness.
>
> — *Romans 12:6–7*

Exercising spiritual gifts. When we are baptized in the Spirit, we receive spiritual gifts, which God has designed for building up the body of Christ. That means he equips us to continue Christ's work of rescuing people and bringing them into the church. I discussed the operation of these gifts in Chapter Six.

I want to mention here that the first gift I received when I prayed for renewal in the Spirit was the gift of praying in tongues. This gift revolutionized my prayer life. It opened me to a deeper experience of worship. And now when I don't know how to intercede for someone, I can pray in tongues and let the Holy Spirit pray for exactly what is needed. Many people who are baptized in the Spirit receive the gift of tongues. For example, Luke reported in the Acts of the Apostles that everyone who received the Spirit spoke in tongues (see Acts 2:4, 10:46, 19:6). And millions of contemporary Catholics and other Christians have received this gift.

Overcoming Obstacles

We may want to pray to be baptized in the Holy Spirit, but feel that obstacles stand in the way. Common blocks are doubt, fear, and a sense of unworthiness.

Doubt. Just before we ask the Lord to renew us in the Spirit, we may imagine that "it could happen for others but maybe not for me." For instance, Bert says that he once suspected that there was an asterisk on the Lord's promise of the Spirit that said "*except Bert Ghezzi."

Fear. Some people hesitate to pray for a release of the Spirit for fear that the Lord may pull a surprise on them. They worry that he may make them give up something that they like or send them somewhere they don't want to go.

Unworthiness. We may feel for some reason that we do not deserve the gift of the Spirit. Perhaps someone may have lived a self-indulgent lifestyle, as I did in my youth. Or maybe a person believes he cannot receive the fullness of the Spirit because he was guilty of serious wrongdoing.

The antidote for all of these obstacles is God's love for us and his unalterable promise of the Holy Spirit summed up in Luke 11:

> **"Ask, and it will be given you; search, and you will find; knock, and the door will be opened for you. For everyone who asks receives, and everyone who searches finds, and for everyone who knocks, the door will be opened. Is there anyone among you, who if your child asks for a fish, will give a snake instead of a fish? Or if the child asks for an egg, will give a scorpion? If you then, who are evil, know how to give good gifts to your children, how much more will the heavenly Father give the Holy Spirit to those who ask him?"**
>
> *— Luke 11:9–13*

God created us to be his daughters and sons. He has always loved us unconditionally.

- Why should we **doubt** our Father's promise to give us the Spirit when he is infinitely more reliable than any human dad?

- Why should we **fear** the Father who loves us, looks out for us, and makes our well-being a high priority? Being baptized in the Spirit is life-changing, but not disruptive.

- We may feel a sense of **unworthiness.** Well, we are all unworthy sinners. No one deserves the gift of the Holy Spirit. God loved us so much that he sent his only Son to the cross to eradicate our sins. We have received his forgiveness. So no reason remains for us not to ask him for the fullness of the Spirit.

If I have not helped you overcome these obstacles, I urge you to talk to the Lord about them. Tell him that you want the release of the Spirit, but have a doubt or a fear. If you feel unworthy or doomed by sin, tell him that you are sorry for what you have done.

Then you can feel as unworthy as you want, but confidently ask him for a release of the Spirit.

Praying for an Outpouring of the Holy Spirit

If you want to pray for being baptized in the Holy Spirit, you can take a number of approaches:

- You may want to have someone pray with you, as Richard did with me. You might discuss this book with several friends and then pray for each other. You could call or email ChristLife (info@Christlife.org; 888-498-8474 or 410-531-7701) to see if any parish near you is offering the Discovering Christ course.

- You may pray on your own, asking the Lord to release the Holy Spirit in your life. Bert says he once shared about the Holy Spirit with a student who returned a week later having been baptized in the Spirit while showering! (You may want to use the prayer that you will find below.)

Deciding to pray for a release of the Spirit is a very serious step. Take your time to consider what you will be doing and what God will be doing for you. You may want to reflect on Scripture (for example, John 14–17; Acts 1–2; Romans 12; 1 Corinthians 12–14; Ephesians 4). You may want to re-read portions of this book. When you are ready, pray with confidence, asking the Lord to baptize you in the Spirit. He will do it.

> **Let us rediscover, dear brothers and sisters, the beauty of being baptized in the Holy Spirit; let us be aware again of our baptism and of our confirmation, sources of grace that are always present.**
>
> *— Pope Benedict XVI*[20]

A Prayer for Renewal in the Spirit

Lord God, I open myself to you. I turn to you and turn away from my sins. Please forgive me for all the things I have done wrong. Jesus, I welcome you as the Lord and Savior of my life. I commit myself to follow you. I ask you, Holy Spirit, to fill me and empower me with your presence and gifts to live as a son/daughter of God. I ask this in the name of the Lord Jesus Christ. And I praise and thank you for hearing my prayer. Amen.

Chapter Eight

New Life in the Spirit: Being a Catholic Disciple

Bert

Following Jesus

At about thirty years of age, Jesus left his home at Nazareth to begin making public appearances in Galilee. Early in his ministry he called men to follow him. His magnetic Spirit attracted Andrew, Simon Peter, James, John, Philip, Nathaniel, and others, who dropped everything to join him. He was assembling a band of companions that he would train to work with him to proclaim the good news. As their rabbi — their teacher — he instructed them in his new way of living and equipped them to carry on his ministry.

"Take my yoke upon you, and learn from me; for I am gentle and humble in heart and you will find rest for your souls. For my yoke is easy, and my burden is light."

— Matthew 11:29–30

Receiving New Life in the Spirit

Bert

In Chapters Six and Seven, Dave and I encouraged you to dedicate yourself to the Lord and to ask him to release the Holy Spirit in your life. Many people who pray in this way immediately experience such things as an intense and intimate presence of God, a sense of awe, a desire to praise God, or a charismatic gift like praying in tongues. Others at first don't experience much at all, but in a short time the Holy Spirit manifests himself to them in some way. They may find themselves wanting to spend time praying. Or they may desire to read Scripture, which seems to have become more meaningful to them than ever before. And they may begin to experience the presence of the Lord in a direct and powerful way.

Many years ago I prayed with a group of friends to be baptized in the Holy Spirit. The others had noticeable experiences, but nothing seemed to happen for me. I believed that the Lord wanted to renew us in the Spirit, but I thought that maybe I was an exception to his promise. But the next day a friend encouraged me to expect the Spirit to act. He urged me to pray and watch for God's touch. In a few days I sensed the Lord's presence lifting me from a longstanding low-level depression. A week later I received the gift of praying in tongues, which revolutionized my prayer life.

I encourage all who pray for a release of the Spirit to expect him to act. Don't let fears and doubts rob you of the Lord's promise. Wait and watch for his gift of new life in the Spirit.

A rabbi's followers were called "disciples" because he *disciplined* them to embrace his teaching and his way of life. He described their accepting his tutelage as taking his "yoke" upon themselves. Rabbi Jesus wanted the same for his disciples. He invited them to take up his yoke and learn from him (see quote on page 91). Jesus intended that they should become like him in every way. He said his "yoke is easy and his burden is light" because he promised to remain with his disciples (see Matthew 28:20). So he would send them the Holy Spirit to activate their new way of living. The Spirit would instruct, equip, and guide them in their work of building the church.

We must view our Spirit-led Christian lives from this same perspective. Jesus' dynamic magnetism draws us to him. He calls each of us to follow him. Jesus wants us to become his disciples. He invites us to apply his teaching to our lives, model our behavior on his, and become transformed in his likeness. He plans to remain with us as we remain in him (see John 15:4). That's why he gives us the Holy Spirit at baptism. And that's why he releases the Spirit afresh in us when we ask to be renewed.

Jesus empowered the original disciples to witness about him throughout the world. He expected them to gather women, men, and children to him and to the church. Now Jesus fills us with the Spirit so that we can continue his work in our worlds. He wants us to collaborate with him in his great rescue operation for all people.

Who Is Your Teacher?

Our response to Jesus' call to discipleship requires a decision to take him as our teacher. That means letting him replace others who may be directing us. We must ask ourselves, "Who is my teacher?" We may be influenced by a parent whose wisdom may be good ("Always be kind!") or bad (Always be first!"). Or we may go along with the crowd, whether to right or to wrong. Most of us identify with teachers who reach us through the media. We take cues from our favorite news commentator, blogger, athlete, or celebrity.

Take a moment to ask who are your teachers? You may have to cancel classes with some of them in order to accept Jesus as your teacher and become his disciple. You will have to test the wisdom of others against his teachings. He wants us to follow the patterns of behavior he taught in the Sermon on the Mount (Matthew 5–7) and his farewell address at the Last Supper (John 13–16). For example, we will become more like our Teacher when we love enemies, forgive offenders, and love sisters and brothers as he loves us. Jesus also wants us to receive the teaching he communicates to us through the church. For instance, he wants us to share his concern for protecting the unborn and serving the poor.

Some of our other teachers may have formed us for ill, promoting bad behaviors. But not to worry — Jesus, our new teacher, has arranged for the Holy Spirit to reform our thinking and transform our lives from the inside out.

"If you love me you will keep my commandments. And I will ask the Father, and he will give you another Advocate, to be with you forever. This is the Spirit of truth, whom the world cannot receive, because it neither sees him nor knows him. You know him, because he abides with you, and will be in you....

"I have said these things to you while I am still with you. But the Advocate, the Holy Spirit, whom the Father will send in my name, will teach you everything, and remind you of all that I have said to you."

— John 14:15–17; 25–26

The Essentials of Christian Growth

God has revealed himself in Christ and has come to dwell in us by the Holy Spirit. He wants to prepare us to be with him forever by growing us up to full maturity in Christ (see Colossians 1:28). That's the work of the Spirit. He is renewing us in the image of God (see Colossians 3:10). He is gradually making us more like Christ (see 2 Corinthians 3:18).

The Lord continuously supplies all the graces we need for growth in the Christian life. And he has given four essential ways to receive the spiritual power that he offers us:

- Prayer and Scripture study
- Service and Evangelization
- The Sacraments
- Community

We will discuss the first two ways here and take up the sacraments and community in the next chapter.

Praying Daily

We are not always aware that God is trying to communicate with us. Yet he stands ready to engage us in a conversation if only we will turn to him in prayer. Our opening to God gives him the opportunity to engineer our spiritual growth. Regular prayer is not an optional extra, like tinted windows in an automobile. Instead, like a car's transmission, it performs an essential function in our Christian life.

Saints and other experienced spiritual advisers say that disciples must pray daily in order to maintain their relationship with the Lord. Many Christians *try* to pray every day, but more often than not they try and fail. Trying just doesn't work. We must decide to make a daily prayer time. And we must build it into our routine at a definite hour of the day. More than four decades ago, both Dave and I made commitments to pray daily and made it a part of our routines. Dave did it in response to a talk by Ralph Martin, a well-known teacher on spirituality. I decided on daily prayer following the example of friends at Duquesne University who were already faithful pray-ers.

Dave and I recommend that you devote fifteen minutes of your prime time each day to prayer. Fill those moments with prayers that you like and that draw you close to God. Those who are Catholic may pray formal prayers like the Our Father, Hail Mary, and Glory Be. You may want to use prayer books like *A Beginner's Book of Prayer* or *Prayer Book for Catholics*, or perhaps a devotional like *The Word Among Us* magazine.[21] You may imitate Dave, who likes to begin his time of prayer singing praise songs. Or you could reflect on one or two Psalms, as I usually do.

But you should also spend time talking to the Lord in your own words — repenting of sins, thanking him for all he has done for you, and interceding for others. And be sure to take time to listen to God, who wants to communicate his love and leadings in the quiet of your heart.

Reading Scripture

God speaks to us in many ways. He encourages us in our thoughts. He gives us good desires to serve him and others. He communicates with us through nature and ordinary events, like conversations with a friend. And God especially speaks to us though the books of the Bible.

I suggest that you devote part of your daily prayer time to reading Scripture. If you are not already an experienced reader of the Bible, I recommend that you start with the New Testament. For example, read Mark, the shortest of the gospels. There you will meet Jesus and come to know him better.

> **All scripture is inspired by God and is useful for teaching, for reproof, for correction, and for training in righteousness, so that everyone who belongs to God may be proficient, equipped for every good work.**
>
> *— 2 Timothy 3:16*

As you read any Scripture text, you should ask two questions. For understanding, ask, "What did the original writer intend to say?" To discover the meaning of the text for your life, ask, "What is the Holy Spirit saying to me through this passage?" If a verse strikes you, pause and think about it. After you have read and reflected on a text, pray about it in your own words.

But don't stop with reading, reflecting, and praying. Once you grasp what the Lord may be saying to you, figure out how you might apply it to your life. Building prayerful reading of Scripture into your daily routine will allow the Holy Spirit to make you a more effective disciple.

Service and Evangelization

When the Holy Spirit comes to us, he brings a variety of gifts that equip us for our service as disciples. We may receive gifts for teaching, encouraging, caring for others, administering, giving generously, and the like. The Spirit works through them for the good of brothers and sisters in the church and the world (see 1 Corinthians 12:7). "Each one of you has received a special grace," said St. Peter, "so, like good stewards responsible for all these varied graces of God, put it at the service of others" (1 Peter 4:10, NJB).

> **On all Christians therefore is laid the splendid burden of working to make the divine message of salvation known and accepted by all men throughout the world.**
>
> — *Vatican Council II,* Decree on the Laity, *3*

All these gifts empower us for evangelization, which Christ has made our primary service as disciples. He has commissioned us to reach out to others and draw them to him and to the church.

Don't let the word "evangelization" put you off. Mainly it means sharing with friends what the Lord has done for you. It's a matter of show and tell.

- **Show.** We pattern our lives on Christ, and our good example intrigues others, who wonder why we behave as we do.
- **Tell.** When friends give us the opportunity, we tell them how the Lord has loved us and given us new life.

Everyday Evangelization

Make evangelization an everyday habit by following these five steps:

1. Decide. Decide that when someone gives you an opportunity, you will share how you came to know the Lord.

2. Pray. Pray daily for specific people in your social environments (family, relatives, friends, coworkers or fellow students, acquaintances).

3. Serve. Conduct your daily life as loving service to others. Doing this will give intriguing Christian witness to people in your social environments.

4. Prepare. Prepare a one-minute testimony or explanation of how you came to know the Lord. You will then be ready to share Christ with others.

5. Tell. At some point in your relationships, individuals will give you an opening to speak to them about the Lord. Example is not enough. You need to take opportunities to share with others how you came to meet Christ.

I learned years ago that if I did not take a deliberate approach to evangelization, I would not do it. So I decided that I would be open about my faith. I would share my Christian experience with anyone who gave me an opportunity. I also decided to pray for people with whom I had some connection as a relative or friend. These decisions have served me well, giving me many occasions to evangelize — and the great pleasure of watching someone I spoke to come to Christ and the church.

Engaging the Holy Spirit with the essentials of spiritual growth makes life exciting — and busy — for twenty-first-century disciples.

Chapter Nine

Community and Sacraments:
Why We Need the Church

Bert

The Disciple's Prayer

The prayer that Jesus taught his original followers has become known as "The Lord's Prayer." I like to call it "The Disciple's Prayer," because it involves us in Christ's mission and asks him to help us fulfill it. Praying "Thy kingdom come" commits us to follow Jesus as his disciples. We are saying that we want to join him in his work of rescuing lost humanity.

Then the prayer petitions the Lord for the graces we need to accomplish our discipleship responsibilities. "Give us this day our daily bread" asks him to strengthen us spiritually for our Christian service. "Forgive us our trespasses" as we forgive our trespassers invokes the Lord's assistance in maintaining and repairing rela-

Our Father, who art in heaven, hallowed be thy name; thy kingdom come; thy will be done on earth as it is in heaven.

Give us this day our daily bread; and forgive us our trespasses as we forgive those who trespass against us; and lead us not into temptation, but deliver us from evil.

Amen.

tionships with our sisters and brothers.

These two petitions express our desire to participate in benefits Jesus arranged for us in his church. He founded the church as a community of men and women who support each other in a love like his that forgives all faults and failures. And he created the sacraments as ways he could give us "our daily bread" — which we can understand as graces for Christian living. Like prayer, Scripture, service, and evangelization, which we discussed in Chapter Eight, community and sacraments are essentials for our growth to Christian maturity.

Community — Why We Need the Church

Assembling people into community with him has always constituted a fundamental element of God's strategy for saving humankind. He began by forming Israel as his special people. And as we saw in Chapter Eight, Jesus initiated his public ministry by calling together a band of men to join his work. Everything he did — preaching, teaching, healing, rebuking evil spirits — served his primary goal of drawing people to himself. Jesus was launching the community of men and women that would extend his ministry throughout the world. After his death and resurrection, he sent the Holy Spirit to them, establishing the church that brings salvation to all humanity.

The Lord does not save us as individuals. He rescues us from our sinful human circumstances by bringing us into his divine family. Jesus used the image of a vine and branches to teach us that new life comes to us only through connectedness to him. He was painting a word picture of the church. He said:

> **[God] has willed to make men holy and save them, not as individuals without any bond or link between them, but rather to make them into a people who might acknowledge him and serve him in holiness.**
>
> — Catechism of the Catholic Church, *781*

"Abide in me as I abide in you. Just as the branch cannot bear fruit by itself unless it abides in the vine, neither can you unless you abide in me. I am the vine, you are the branches. Those who abide in me and I in them bear much fruit, because apart from me you can do nothing" (John 15:4–5).

St. Paul also described the church as a living organism. He says that at baptism the Holy Spirit incorporates us into the body of Christ. Jesus governs the body as its head, and we serve as its members. Just as the members of the human body work together, we must collaborate with the other members of the church to accomplish what God wants of us (see 1 Corinthians 12:12–26).

So we need the church because the Lord designed it as his way of giving us new life. He knew that we would depend on brothers and sisters to support us. He wanted us to make friends with whom we could pray and honestly share our lives. And the church needs us to collaborate with Christ in his great rescue operation.

Experiencing Community

I did not experience the church as a community until I became a young adult. But ever since my initial involvement in Christian groups, relationships with brothers and sisters have been an indispensible support for me. As a college student I linked up with friends who influenced me to give my life to Christ. Praying, sharing Scripture, and serving with them occasioned my choosing to become a disciple. Over the years Mary Lou, my wife, and I participated in a series of communities that sustained our Christian life and helped us grow spiritually. We were baptized in the Holy Spirit among brothers and sisters at Notre Dame. Then as we moved from Indiana through Michigan to Florida, in every place we drew strength from communities. We still rely on friends we made in Christian family groups, prayer groups, a covenant community, and parish ministries.

Participation in Christian community also provides us opportunities to discover and exercise our gifts. The Lord gives each of us gifts, and they come in great varieties. When we gather in community, these gifts work together for the benefit of all. One brings a gift for teaching, another for encouraging, and a third for evangelizing; one is gifted for reaching out to the homeless, another for caring for the sick, and a third for advancing prolife causes. As we exercise our gifts, they generate new life not only for the members of the community but for the people we meet every day in our worlds.

If you are involved in a Christian community, whatever gifts you bring, give them generously. If you are not participating in a community, look for one that will not only help you grow, but will also give you an opportunity to discover and use your gifts. You may benefit from participating in more than one faith community.

The Sacraments

Jesus became a man just like us in every way except sin. He knew firsthand what we humans are like. He recognized that we would find living as his disciples difficult.

When we attempt to put the gospel into practice, we often experience a frustrating interior struggle. We desire in our hearts to follow Christ's teachings and commands, but somehow we can't always make our choices and actions conform to them. Jesus put his finger on our dilemma when he said, "The spirit indeed is willing, but the flesh is weak" (Matthew 26:41). Twenty

> **"Pray that you may not come into the time of trial; the spirit indeed is willing, but the flesh is weak."**
>
> — *Matthew 26:41*

years after his conversion to Christ, this same tension between desire and behavior still troubled St. Paul. He said, "I do not do what I want, but I do the very thing I hate" (Romans 7:15).

Jesus did not expect us to overcome this fundamental human weakness on our own. He made arrangements so that he could be present to us and empower us for Christian living. We call these arrangements "sacraments."

The Lord designed the sacraments to fortify our spirits. Since he had created us as spirits encased in bodies, he had to reach them through our senses. So he gave the sacraments signs that we could see, touch, taste, and hear. For example, water signifies baptism; bread and wine, the Eucharist; sealing with oil, confirmation and anointing of the sick, and so on. None of these signs have any sacramental power on their own. The Lord acts through them to accomplish in us what they signify to our senses.

The Lord did not create the sacraments as vending machines that dispense his graces. He made them doorways through which we go to seek him for spiritual nourishment, forgiveness, strengthening, and support. Jesus does not just give gifts and graces to meet our needs and then step back from us. In the sacraments he comes to us in person. Jesus gives us himself as food, healing, mercy, and strength. They are the primary ways we as disciples experience union with our Master and receive from him the spiritual benefits of his risen life. For example:

- Baptism is the sacrament that initiates us into the Christian life. It frees us from sin and connects us to the body of Christ, the church.

- The Eucharist gives us nourishment and strength for daily Christian living. Jesus himself comes to us through the sacramental signs of bread and wine.

- Reconciliation is the sacrament that gives us the opportunity to receive forgiveness of sins by confessing them to Jesus in the priest who represents him.

- Marriage unites a man and a woman for their mutual good and support and for the procreation and education of children.

- The Anointing of the Sick produces spiritual strength and endurance for the ill and aging and may bring physical healing.

The last two chapters presented the basic responses we must make to receive the abundant graces that come with new life in the Spirit. To tap into the power that God offers we must faithfully engage the four essentials for our Christian growth:

- Schedule prayer and Scripture study into our daily routine;

- Work with Christ in service and evangelization;

- Involve ourselves with brothers and sisters in a Christian community;

- Receive the sacraments, especially Penance and the Eucharist.

We will not succeed if we *try* to practice these basics or if we apply them one at a time. The four essentials work together to bring us the transforming power of the Spirit. We must decide to do all four. If we neglect any one of them, we will be depriving ourselves of the spiritual energy we need for effective Christian living.

You can count on Dave's and my daily prayers as you open yourself more fully to the Lord. May you come to know him more clearly, love him more dearly, and follow him more nearly every day.

Invitations to Our Readers

Dave and I know that you, our readers, come from different backgrounds and find yourselves in diverse circumstances. We want each of you to enter a personal relationship with Jesus and to receive new life in the Spirit. We also want you to connect with the Lord as a member of his body, the church. So we offer the following invitations.

- We suggest that Catholics who participate actively in the church review your involvements and ask God what he wants of you now.

- We urge inactive Catholics to consider joining a parish. Call a local pastor, ask about inquiry opportunities, investigate informative classes, and inquire about programs such as the Rite of Christian Initiation for Adults (RCIA). Read books like Frank Sheed's *A Map of Life*, which is a basic study of Catholicism. Consult www.Catholicscomehome.org and www.catholic.com with your questions and concerns.

- We invite former Catholics to seek resolution of any grievance with a local pastor, a diocesan representative, or a qualified lay person. Look for ways to forgive anyone in the church who has offended you. Consider participating in an informative parish program. Read books like Frank Sheed's *A Map of Life*, which is a basic study of Catholicism. Consult www.Catholicscomehome.org and www.catholic.com with your questions and concerns.

- We invite unchurched readers to explore membership in the church. Take your questions to a priest or lay leader at a nearby Catholic parish. Attend, without obligation, inquiry or informative presentations at the parish. Read books like Thomas Merton's *The Seven Storey Mountain*. Explore websites like Fr. Robert Barron's wordonfire.org and Jennifer Fulwiler's conversiondiary.com. If you are not baptized, when ready, speak to a priest or lay leader about how to proceed.

- We invite Christians who belong to other churches to reflect on the message of *Discover Christ.* And we encourage you to make or renew a personal commitment to Christ and ask him to release the Holy Spirit afresh in your life.

Recommended Reading

Bert Ghezzi, *Adventures in Daily Prayer.* Grand Rapids, MI: Brazos Press, 2010.

Peter Herbeck, *When the Spirit Comes in Power.* Cincinnati, OH: Servant Books, 2003.

C. S. Lewis. *Mere Christianity* (various editions).

C. S. Lewis. *The Screwtape Letters* (various editions).

Jacquelyn Lindsey. *Catholic Pocket Prayer Book.* Huntington, IN: Our Sunday Visitor, 2002.

George Martin. *Reading God's Word Today: A Practical and Faith-filled Approach to Scripture.* Huntington, IN: Our Sunday Visitor, 2009.

Thomas Merton. *The Seven Storey Mountain* (various editions).

Alan Schreck, *Catholic and Christian: An Explanation of Commonly Misunderstood Catholic Beliefs.* Cincinnati, OH: Servant Books, 2004.

Frank Sheed. *A Map of Life: A Simple Study of the Catholic Faith.* San Francisco: Ignatius Press, 1994.

Frank Sheed. *To Know Christ Jesus.* San Francisco: Ignatius Press, 1992.

William G. Storey. *A Beginner's Book of Prayer.* Chicago: Loyola Press, 2009.

The Word Among Us, a monthly magazine of daily meditations. Order at www.wau.org or call 1-800-775-9673.

Endnotes

1 In "Quotable Quotes," *Readers Digest* (March, 2006) 81.

2 Fr. Larry Richards, *Be a Man* (San Francisco: Ignatius Press, 2009), 12.

3 Leo Tolstoy, *The Confession,* Part V (www.mnstate.edu/gracyk/courses/web%20publishing/TolstoyConfession.htm; translation in the public domain, source consulted February 11, 2011).

4 Frank Sheed, *The Map of Life* (San Francisco, CA: Ignatius Press, 1994), 12.

5 www.myfoxorlando.com/dpp/news/volusia_news/100209_Child_finds_grenade_in_Daytona_Beach consulted February 11, 2011.

6 C. S. Lewis, *Mere Christianity* (San Francisco, CA: HarperCollins, 2001), 52.

7 C. S. Lewis, *The Screwtape Letters* (New York: Macmillan, 1982), 11.

8 David Popenoe, *Life without Father* (New York: The Free Press, 1996), 2–3.

9 Bert Ghezzi, *Adventures in Daily Prayer* (Grand Rapids, MI: Brazos Press, 2010), 89-90.

10 C. S. Lewis, *Mere Christianity* in *The Complete C. S. Lewis Signature Classics* (New York: HarperCollins, 2002), 35.

11 G. K. Chesterton, *Orthodoxy* (New York: Doubleday, 2001), 9.

12 Adapted from Bert Ghezzi, *Adventures in Daily Prayer* (Grand Rapids, MI: Brazos Press, 2010), 44–45.

13 Adapted from *Summa Theologica,* III, 53. 1.

14 F. J. Sheed, *Theology for Beginners* (Ann Arbor, MI: Servant Books, 1981), 27.

15 Peter Herbeck, *When the Spirit Comes in Power* (Ann Arbor, MI: Servant Books, 2003), 62–64.

16 On the Holy Spirit, a catechetical instruction by St. Cyril of Jerusalem (ca. 315–386) in *The Office of Readings According to the Roman Rite*; trans. the International Commission on English in the Liturgy (Boston: Daughters of St. Paul, 1983), 629–630.

17 Bert Ghezzi, *Adventures in Daily Prayer* (Grand Rapids, MI, 2010), 50.

18 Peter Cardinal Turkson, quoted in a Times of London interview at www.timesonline.co.uk/tol/comment/faith/article2795329.ece>.

19 St. Louis de Montfort, *True Devotion to the Blessed Virgin*, #127 at www.montfort.org.uk/Writings/TrueDev.html.

20 Pope Benedict XVI, Regina Caeli Address, Pentecost Sunday, May 11, 2008.

21 William G. Storey, *A Beginner's Book of Prayer* is available at www.loylolapress.com. Jaquelyn Lindsey, *Prayer Book for Catholics* is available at www.osv.com. *The Word Among Us* is a monthly devotional magazine that offers reflections on the Scriptures read at daily Mass (www.wau.org).

NOTES

NOTES

NOTES

NOTES

NOTES

NOTES

NOTES

NOTES

NOTES

Parish and Small-Group Resources

Discovering Christ
on DVD!

Take your experience of *Discover Christ* to the next
level by participating in the DVD-based *Discovering
Christ* series in a parish or small group.

Experience the Gospel coming alive as you watch the presentations and engage in meaningful discussions on the teachings.

To purchase *Discovering Christ* or find a *Discovering Christ* course near you, visit www.christlife.org/discover or call toll-free 1-888-498-8474.

If this book has helped you enter into a personal relationship with the Lord Jesus, we would love to hear from you. You can contact us at info@christlife.org.

The content of *Discover Christ* was developed by ChristLife, a Catholic ministry of the Archdiocese of Baltimore. ChristLife's mission is to help others discover, follow, and share Jesus Christ in the Catholic Church.

ChristLife equips dioceses, parishes, small groups, and young adults with an evangelizing process. ChristLife's three major programs are: *Discovering Christ*, *Following Christ*, and *Sharing Christ*. To find out more about these and other resources, contact us:

ChristLife   12280 Folly Quarter Rd.
Ellicott City, MD 20142
Web: www.christlife.org
Email: info@christlife.org
Phone: 1-888-498-8474